6g   A Review *92*
6h   An Abstract from *Dissertation Abstracts International* *92*
6i   A Secondary Source *93*

Audiovisual Sources *94*

7a   A Film *94*
7b   A Filmstrip *95*
7c   A Television Broadcast *95*
7d   A Radio Broadcast *96*
7e   A Recording *96*
7f   A Performance *97*
7g   An Interview *97*
7h   A Transcript *98*
7i   A Lecture or Speech *98*
7j   A Work of Art *98*
7k   An Exhibit *99*
7l   A Map, Graph, Table, or Chart *99*
7m   A Cartoon *100*

Electronic Sources *101*

8a   An Online Scholarly Project, Information Database, or Professional Web Site *103*
8b   A Source from an Online Scholarly Project, Information Database, or Professional Web Site *103*
8c   An Online Book *104*
8d   An Article in an Online Journal *104*
8e   An Article in an Online Magazine *105*
8f   An Article in an Online Newspaper *105*
8g   An Article in an Online Encyclopedia or Other Reference Work *106*
8h   An Online Government Document *106*
8i   An Online Transcript of a Lecture or Speech *107*
8j   An Online Work of Art *107*
8k   An Online Exhibit *108*
8l   An Online Map, Graph, Table, or Chart *108*
8m   An Online Transcript of a Television or Radio Broadcast *108*
8n   An Online Audio Source *109*
8o   A CD-ROM Source *109*
8p   An E-mail Interview *109*
8q   An Online Posting *110*

Pocket Guide to the Chicago Manual of Style

FIRST EDITION

Robert Perrin
Indiana State University

HOUGHTON MIFFLIN COMPANY
Boston   New York

161089

Publisher: Patricia A. Coryell
Senior Sponsoring Editor: Lisa Kimball
Assistant Editor: Jane Acheson
Project Editor: Aimee Chevrette
Editorial Assistant: Andrew Laskey
Senior Art and Design Coordinator: Jill Haber Atkins
Photo Editor: Jennifer Meyer Dare
Composition Buyer: Chuck Dutton
Manufacturing Buyer: Susan Brooks
Senior Marketing Manager: Tom Ziolkowski
Marketing Assistant: Bettina Chiu

Cover image: © Hulton-Deutsch Collection/CORBIS

Printed in the U.S.A.

Library of Congress Control Number: 2006935673

Instructor's exam copy:
ISBN-13: 978-0-618-83300-9
ISBN-10: 0-618-83300-5

For orders, use student text ISBNs:
ISBN-13: 978-0-618-76723-6
ISBN-10: 0-618-76723-1

456789-DOC-10 09 08

Z
253
P47
2007

Contents

Preface   xi

1   **Writing Scholarly Papers**   1

     1a   Subject and Topic   1
        Guidelines for Assessing General Subjects   1
        Narrow Topic   2
     1b   Thesis Statements, Hypotheses,
        or Stated Objectives   2
        Thesis Statement   2
        Hypothesis   3
        Stated Objective   3
     1c   Research Goals   3
        Course-Related Goals   3
        Professional Goals   4
        Personal Goals   5
     1d   Research Methods   5
        Library-Based Research   5
        Online Catalogs and Periodical Databases   6
           Information about Books (and Other
              Library-Based Materials)   6
           Information about Periodicals   7
        Internet-Based Research   8
     1e   Evaluating Sources   9
        Print Sources   9
        Audiovisual Sources   10
        Internet Sources   10
        Combinations of Sources   12
     1f   Note-Taking   13
        Methods of Note-Taking   13
        Complete Information   13
        Consistent Format   14
        Kinds of Notes   14
     1g   Plagiarism   15
        Common Knowledge   16
        Special Qualities of Source Materials   17
     1h   Planning   20
        Reviewing Notes   20
        Thesis Statement or Stated Objective   20
        An Informal Outline   20
        A Formal Outline   20

1i Writing Strategies   21
        General Strategies for Drafting a Paper   21
        Strategies for Drafting a Research Paper   22
        Questions for Revising Content   23
        Questions for Revising Style   23
        Questions for Revising Technical Matters   24

2 Preparing Chicago-Style Manuscripts   25

2a Parts of the Manuscript   25
        Title page   25
        List of Illustrations   27
        List of Tables   29
        The Text   31
        Appendixes   32
        Endnotes   32
        Glossary   33
        Bibliography   34
2b General Manuscript Guidelines   35
        Paper   34
        Font Selection   34
        Line Spacing   35
        Margins and Indentations   35
        Paging   35
        Titles and Headings for Sections   36
        Submitting the Paper   36
        Order of the Manuscript   37

3 Following Chicago Editorial Style   38

3a Punctuation and Mechanics   38
        Periods   38
        Commas   39
        Semicolons   40
        Colons   40
        Question Marks   41
        Exclamation Points   42
        Hyphens   42
        Dashes   42
        Parentheses   43
        Brackets   44
        Slashes   44
        Quotation Marks   45
        Ellipsis Points   45
        Capitalization   46
        Italics   48

Number Style   49
    Cardinal and Ordinal Numbers   52
    Commas in Numbers   52
    Plurals of Numbers   52
    Inclusive Numbers   53
3b   General Style   51
Transitions   53
Verb Tense   54
Agreement   55
Parallelism   57
3c   Word Choice   57
Noun Clusters   58
Jargon   58
Colloquialisms   58
Specificity   59
Biased Language   59
    Racial and Ethnic Bias   59
    Gender Bias   60
    Other Forms of Bias   61

4   **Preparing Endnotes, Footnotes, and the Bibliography**   62

4a   Endnotes and Footnotes—
An Overview   62
4b   Placing Note Numbers in the Paper   62
4c   Information for Endnotes and
Footnotes   63
4d   Format for Endnotes and Footnotes   65
4e   Positioning Endnotes and Footnotes   66
4f   Multiple Notes from the Same Source   66
The Same Source—Consecutive Notes   66
The Same Source—
Nonconsecutive Notes   67
4g   Multiple References in the Same Note   67
4h   The Bibliography—An Overview   67
4i   Information for Bibliographic Entries   67
4j   Format for Bibliographic Entries   68
4k   Alphabetizing the Bibliography   68
4l   Specialized Elements of a Bibliography   70
Distinct Elements in Bibliographies   70
    Multiple Works by Same Author   70
    Four or More Authors or Editors   70
    Authors Using Pseudonyms   70
Annotated Bibliographies   71

viii   Contents

4m Quotations   71
        Brief Prose Quotations (Fewer than One
        Hundred Words)   72
        Brief Verse Quotations (One or Two Lines)   72
        Long Prose Quotations
        (One Hundred Words or More)   73
        Long Verse Quotations
        (Three or More Lines)   74
        Punctuation with Quotations   74

5   Preparing Note Forms for Books and
        Other Separately Published Materials   77

5a A Book by One Author   78
5b A Book by Two or Three Authors   78
5c A Book by Four or More Authors   78
5d A Book with No Author Named   79
5e A Book by an Author Using a Pseudonym   79
5f A Book with an Organization as Author   79
5g An Edition Other than the First   80
5h A Revised or Enlarged Edition   80
5i A Reprinted Book   80
5j A Multivolume Work   80
5k An Edited Collection   81
5l A Selection in an Edited Collection   81
5m Multiple References to the Same
        Collection   82
5n An Article in an Encyclopedia or Other
        Reference Work   82
5o A Work in a Series   82
5p An Imprint   83
5q A Translation   83
5r A Government Document—*Congressional
        Record*   84
5s A Government Document—Committee,
        Commission, Department   84
5t A Preface, Introduction, Foreword,
        Epilogue, or Afterword   85
5u A Pamphlet or Brochure   86
5v Published Proceedings from a
        Conference   86
5w A Dissertation   86
5x A Book Written in a Language Other
        than English   87
5y Sacred Writings   87
5z A Secondary Source   88

6 Preparing Note Forms for Periodicals   89

   6a An Article in a Journal with Continuous
           Paging   89
   6b An Article in a Journal with Separate
           Paging   90
   6c An Article in a Monthly Magazine   91
   6d An Article in a Weekly Magazine   91
   6e An Article in a Newspaper   91
   6f An Editorial or a Letter to the Editor   92
   6g A Review   92
   6h An Abstract from Dissertation Abstracts
           International   92
   6i A Secondary Source   93

7 Preparing Note Forms for Audiovisual
       Sources   94

   7a A Film   94
   7b A Filmstrip   95
   7c A Television Broadcast   95
   7d A Radio Broadcast   96
   7e A Recording   96
   7f A Performance   97
   7g An Interview   97
   7h A Transcript   98
   7i A Lecture or Speech   98
   7j A Work of Art   98
   7k An Exhibit   99
   7l A Map, Graph, Table, or Chart   99
   7m A Cartoon   100

8 Preparing Note Forms for
       Electronic Sources   101

   8a An Online Scholarly Project, Information
           Database, or Professional Website   103
   8b A Source from an Online Scholarly Project,
           Information Database, or Professional
           Website   103
   8c An Online Book   104
   8d An Article in an Online Journal   104
   8e An Article in an Online Magazine   105
   8f An Article in an Online Newspaper   105
   8g An Article in an Online Encyclopedia
           or Other Reference Source   106
   8h An Online Government Document   106

8i   An Online Transcript of a Lecture
or Speech   107
8j   An Online Work of Art   107
8k   An Online Exhibit   108
8l   An Online Map, Graph, Table,
or Chart   108
8m An Online Transcript of a Television
or Radio Broadcast   108
8n   An Online Audio Source   109
8o   A CD-ROM Source   109
8p   An E-mail Interview   109
8q   An Online Posting   110

9   Examining a Sample Paper   111

Sample Paper: "Walking into History:
The Legacy of the Lincoln Memorial"
(Jarah Estes-Cooper)   111

Appendixes   127

A   Parts of the Chicago-Style Paper   127
B   Chicago-Style Abbreviations   129
C   Sample Pages   131
D   Bibliographic Entries   136

Index   137

Preface

Pocket Guide to the Chicago Manual of Style is designed for students who need to write, document, and present papers in University of Chicago's endnote or footnote style. This convenient and easy-to-use guide draws on the principles described in the fifteenth edition of *The Chicago Manual of Style* (2003). What sets *Pocket Guide to the Chicago Manual of Style* apart from that lengthy manual is its overriding goal: this text presents the principles in a brief, yet complete and easy-to-use manner. The guide is ideal for undergraduates who are working with Chicago style for the first time. Yet graduate students and working professionals will also appreciate its user-friendliness. To enhance use, *Pocket Guide to the Chicago Manual of Style* incorporates these helpful features:

- *Handbook Format* To make information easy to find, *Pocket Guide* presents major principles in each chapter as numbered precepts (statements of key ideas).

- *Student Focus* Clear explanations and numerous examples make *Pocket Guide* a convenient resource for upper-division undergraduates and beginning graduate students.

- *Writing Scholarly Papers: An Overview* *Pocket Guide*'s introductory chapter describes basic researching and writing methods, serving as a brief review.

- *Manuscript Preparation* In one coherent chapter, *Pocket Guide* describes and illustrates major elements of a Chicago-style manuscript.

- *Editorial Style* In one convenient chapter, *Pocket Guide* explains Chicago-style guidelines for punctuation and mechanics (periods, quotation marks, capitalization, number style, and so on), general writing style (transitions, verb tense, and so on), and word choice (jargon, biased language, and so on).

- *Separate Documentation Chapters* For easy use, *Pocket Guide* provides separate chapters to explain reference-list entries for books, periodicals, audiovisual sources, and electronic sources.

- *Endnotes and Footnotes Samples* One-hundred forty-nine separate sample notes in chapters 4–8 illustrate the principles of documentation in *Pocket Guide.*

- *Tables, Charts, and Textboxes* Throughout *Pocket Guide,* tables, charts, and textboxes present material in easy-to-review formats.

- *Sample Paper* An annotated sample paper is included in *Pocket Guide* to illustrate manuscript form and issues of writing.

- *Discussion of Plagiarism* With its student focus, *Pocket Guide* includes a discussion of plagiarism and ways to avoid it.

- *Appendixes* *Pocket Guide* includes four appendixes: Appendix A briefly describes all elements of a Chicago-style paper, Appendix B provides standard abbreviations, Appendix C includes samples of special features (a list of illustrations, a list of tables, a table, a glossary, and several pages illustrating text pages with footnotes), and Appendix D includes samples of bibliographic entries matched to the reference-note samples in chapters 5–8.

ACKNOWLEDGMENTS

My work on *Pocket Guide* was pleasant and productive because of the supportive, knowledgeable staff at Houghton Mifflin. I especially appreciate Suzanne Phelps Weir's and Lisa Kimball's commitment to this project, Jane Acheson's informed editorial assistance, and Aimee Chevrette's thoughtful and careful handling of production work.

I am also indebted to both the Copyeditor, Karen Osborne, and the Proofreader, Lisa Goodman, for their thoughtful reviews of the revised manuscript of *Pocket Guide to the Chicago Manual of Style.*

Finally, I wish to thank Judy, Jenny, Chris, and Kate for their encouragement.

R. P.

1   Writing Scholarly Papers

1   Writing Scholarly Papers

The research process is a complex combination of thinking, searching, reading, evaluating, writing, and revising. It is, in many ways, a highly personal process because writers approach research activities drawing on different skills and past experiences. Yet researchers often follow a series of connected phases (which nonetheless occur in different order for different people).

This chapter reviews, in a brief way, the common steps that most researchers go through; if you are an experienced researcher, use this chapter as a "refresher." If your research experiences are limited, consider each discussion carefully as you proceed with your work.

1a   Subject and Topic

Research begins with a subject. In some academic contexts, you may choose the subject yourself, usually with the instructor's approval. But in other contexts, you may be required to choose from a small number of topics or be assigned a topic with a predetermined focus.

GUIDELINES FOR ASSESSING GENERAL SUBJECTS

As you select potential subjects for your research (broad categories like architectural conservation, test anxiety, the effects of trade policies, and so on), keep these important and practical principles in mind:

- *Interest.*   When possible, select a subject that interests you. Do not spend time researching a subject that you are not curious about.
- *Length.*   Select a subject that can be adequately treated in the length requirements of the assignment. You may have to expand or reduce the scope of your subject to match an assignment's length requirements.
- *Materials.*   Select a subject for which you can find materials of the kind spelled out in the assignment. Be aware that you can use libraries other than your own

and that the Internet provides access to a broad range of materials, both traditional and nontraditional.

- *Challenge.* Select a subject that challenges you but that does not require technical or other specialized knowledge you may not have time to acquire.

- *Uniqueness.* Select a subject that is not overused. Overly familiar subjects create little interest, and materials are soon depleted.

- *Perspective.* Select a subject you can approach in a fresh, interesting way. Readers will appreciate your efforts to examine subjects in new ways.

NARROW TOPIC

In most instances, you need to narrow your large subject (migrant education, for example) to a specific topic (migrant education in Texas) so that you can both research selectively and address an issue in a focused way.

To discover ways in which to narrow a broad subject to a specific topic, skim general reference materials, paying particular attention to recurrent themes, details, and ideas. Then consider establishing a focus using selected strategies for limiting topics:

- *Time.* Restrict the subject to a specific, manageable time span. For example: School violence in the 1950s.

- *Place.* Restrict the subject to a specific location. For example: Jazz in St. Louis or New Orleans.

- *Special circumstance.* Restrict the subject to a specific context or circumstance. For example: WPA support for the arts.

- *Specific population.* Restrict the subject to address its effects on a selected group of people. For example: Music therapy for the elderly.

1b Thesis Statements, Hypotheses, or Stated Objectives

To clarify the central goal of your writing, present your ideas in one of three alternative ways.

THESIS STATEMENT

A thesis statement, sometimes called a problem statement, is a declarative statement (usually one but sometimes two or more sentences) that clarifies your specific topic, presents your opinion of (not merely facts about) the topic, and incorporates qualifications or limitations necessary to understand your views.

> Although laws governing architectural conservation are well intended, they often drive businesses away from the areas of cities most in need of capital investment.

HYPOTHESIS

A hypothesis is a conjectural statement that guides an argument or investigation; it can be explored (and potentially proved or disproved) by examining data related to your topic. Conditional in nature, a hypothesis is a statement to be assessed using available information.

> Students who delay work on major research projects until the last week are more likely to plagiarize than are students who begin their work early.

STATED OBJECTIVE

A stated objective is a brief, well-focused statement that describes a research paper that presents information. Unsubtle and not arguable, it must define the topic clearly and narrow the topic when necessary.

> I will share a brief history of polio in the United States, ranging from early epidemics to the last recorded American case.

1c Research Goals

Although most research is prompted by specific academic or job-related requirements, you should also think broadly about the goals for your work, recognizing that research provides multifaceted learning experiences.

COURSE-RELATED GOALS

Course-related goals are broad in nature and establish the foundation of your research work.

- *Using the library.* Library-based research should take advantage of a full range of sources, as well as the electronic means to locate them (see pages 6–8).

- *Using the Internet for academic purposes.* Research requires that you learn to use the Internet selectively for scholarly purposes, which means learning to evaluate the credibility and value of online materials (see pages 10–12).
- *Assessing source materials.* In a global way, research depends on critically evaluating materials to ensure that you use sources that credibly support your ideas (see pages 9–13).
- *Taking notes.* Research requires you to record ideas and information from your sources carefully and completely so that you can use them appropriately in your writing (see pages 13–15).
- *Responding effectively to opposing views.* Fair-minded research acknowledges and uses opposing views to create balance in writing (see pages 12–13).
- *Synthesizing ideas.* Effective research blends information and ideas from a variety of sources, thereby creating a comprehensive presentation that is, in some way, better or fairer or clearer than the presentation in individual sources (see pages 12–13).
- *Incorporating material into writing.* Effective research leads to writing that incorporates ideas and information with clarity, accuracy, and style (see pages 71–76).
- *Citing sources accurately.* Research requires that you give proper credit to the people whose ideas and information you have used; this technically focused process requires attention to detail (see chapters 4–8).

PROFESSIONAL GOALS

Professional goals develop from the process of establishing a working knowledge in your field of study. As such, they focus on specific skills and knowledge.

- *Learning to use specific sources.* Research in each discipline requires familiarity with kinds of sources that are respected and commonly used.
- *Using specialized formats.* Each discipline's research incorporates unique formats that you must learn to follow.
- *Using specialized writing styles.* Research in each discipline depends on specific stylistic patterns for presenting ideas and information.
- *Demonstrating discipline-specific knowledge.* Research in each discipline builds upon accepted information that you must be able to incorporate fluently.

PERSONAL GOALS

Personal goals concentrate on degrees of knowledge, improvement, sophistication, and experience. Although they are less easily quantifiable than goals matched to courses, they are equally important.

- *Learning about a subject.* Exploring a subject through research improves your knowledge of your chosen discipline.
- *Improving skills.* Current research gives you the opportunity not only to use your early research work but also to develop more sophisticated skills.
- *Expanding experiences.* Research work allows for varied kinds of personal growth.

1d Research Methods

Methods of research vary depending on the project, but most projects require multidimensional work with a variety of sources. To complete such projects, take advantage of a full range of strategies.

LIBRARY-BASED RESEARCH

Learn to use all the features of your library, especially familiarizing yourself with the research areas that you will most commonly use:

- *Reference.* The collection of general source materials—dictionaries, fact books, encyclopedias, indexes, guides, bibliographies, and so on—that can guide your preliminary research (many of which are now available in electronic form)
- *Catalog (computer).* The cluster of computers where you secure the informational records of library materials
- *Stacks.* The bookcases where print materials (books, bound periodicals, and so on) are stored according to a classification system
- *Current periodicals.* The collection of recent copies of journals, magazines, and newspapers (many of which are now available in electronic form)
- *Government documents.* The collection of printed materials from national, state, and local government departments and agencies—books, monographs, pamphlets, reports, and so on (many of which are also available in electronic form through government Web sites)

- *Microforms.*   The collection of microfilm and microfiche materials
- *Media.*   The collection of audiovisual sources—films, videos, DVDs, CDs, and so on
- *New books.*   The area where new books are displayed before being placed in the general collection
- *Special collections.*   The area where rare books, archival materials, and other special materials are located
- *Special libraries.*   The discipline-specific collections that are housed in sublibraries

ONLINE CATALOGS AND PERIODICAL DATABASES

Online catalogs (also called electronic search systems) allow you to gather technical information on books, monographs, government documents, and other materials in the library's collection; periodical databases (online "indexes") allow you to gather technical information about—and very often secure full texts of—articles in journals, magazines, and newspapers. Both online catalogs and periodical databases provide access to descriptive material about sources when using keyword search techniques.

Keyword searching uses easily recognizable words and phrases (often in combination) to access sources. Computer systems search for keywords in titles, tables of contents, and other descriptive source information and then display "matches." To locate a broad range of materials, use alternative phrases (*collaborative learning, group projects, collaboration, team research,* and so on) as you conduct your searches. Also explore Library of Congress listings, available online at most libraries, to discover unique category descriptions. For example, the Library of Congress system does not use the fairly conventional expression *medical ethics;* rather, its category notation is *medicine—moral and ethical aspects.*

Information about Books (and Other Library-Based Materials)

All online catalogs provide standardized information about each source in the library's collection.

- *Author.*   The full name of the author (or authors)
- *Title.*   The selection's full title, including subtitles

- *Facts of publication.* The city, publisher, and copyright date
- *Technical description.* Specific features—number of pages, book size, and so on
- *Location.* The location of the source in the library's collection or in a special library or collection
- *Call number.* The classification number assigned to the source (indicating where the source is located in the library's collection)
- *Number of items.* The number of items (three volumes, one volume with CD-ROM, and so on), if more than one item exists
- *Status.* Information on whether the source is checked out, on reserve, on loan, and so on
- *Editions.* Descriptions of editions (second, third, revised, enlarged, and so on)
- *Notes.* Descriptions of special features (bibliography, index, appendixes, and so on)
- *Table of contents.* A listing of chapters and section titles and subtitles
- *Subject classification.* The Library of Congress classification, both primary and secondary

Information about Periodicals

Periodical databases provide standardized information about articles in journals, magazines, and newspapers. They also provide articles in a variety of formats.

- *Article title.* The article's full title and subtitle (listed first because some articles have no attributed author)
- *Author.* The full name of the author (or authors)
- *Periodical title.* The title of the journal, magazine, or newspaper
- *City.* The city of publication
- *Date.* The month/year, day/month/year, or season/year of publication
- *Volume and issue number.* The volume (which indicates the number of years a periodical has been published) and number (which indicates the numbers of issues published each year) for journals and magazines, but not newspapers
- *Start page.* The page on which the article begins

- *Number of pages.*   The article's total number of pages (in the original print format)
- *Formats for articles.*   The formats available for selected articles: citation/abstract, full text, page image (see below)

Formats for Articles
(within a Periodical Database)

- *Citation/abstract:*   Technical information, plus an abstract (a brief summary of the ideas in an article)
- *Full text:*   Technical information and abstract, plus the full text of an article in typed form
- *Page image:*   Technical information and abstract, plus scanned images of an article as it appeared in the periodical (often as a PDF file)

INTERNET-BASED RESEARCH

Your Internet search may lead you to a scholarly project (a university-based, scholarly site that makes a wide range of materials—such as full-text books, research data, visual materials—available to researchers), an information database (a site that makes statistical information from governmental agencies, research institutions, or nonprofit corporations available to researchers), or a Web site (a site designed to share information, forward a political agenda, promote a product, advocate a position, or share ideas).

To navigate an Internet site successfully, and to gather crucial information for a reference note or bibliographic entry, learn about the key elements of an Internet home page.

- *Electronic address (URL).*   The "universal (or uniform) resource locator"—the combination of elements that locate the source (for example, http://nasad.arts-accredit.org/ is the URL for the Web site of the National Association of Schools of Art and Design [NASAD])
- *Official title.*   The title and subtitle of the site
- *Author, host, editor, or Web master.*   The name of the person (or people) responsible for the development and maintenance of the site

- *Affiliation or sponsorship.*   The person, group, organization, or agency that develops and maintains the material on the site
- *Location.*   The place (city, school, organization, agency, and so on) where the site originates
- *Posting date or update.*   The date on which the site was first posted or the date of its most recent update (revision)
- *"About This Site."*   A description of how the site was developed, a rationale for it, or information about those involved with the site
- *Site directory.*   An electronic table of contents for the site

1e   Evaluating Sources

Because not all sources are equally useful, you should analyze them and select the best ones, an ongoing process with continued assessments and reassessments.

PRINT SOURCES

Print sources—journals, magazines, newspapers, books, and others—have traditionally been the mainstay of most research. Consequently, they are the easiest to evaluate because of their familiarity.

- *Author's credentials.*   Determine whether an author's academic degrees, scholarly training, affiliations, or other published work establish his or her authority.
- *Appropriate focus.*   Determine whether the source addresses the topic in a way that is matched to your emphasis. Consider literature reviews to establish scholarly context and empirical studies to incorporate recent primary research.
- *Sufficient coverage.*   Determine whether the source sufficiently covers the topic by examining its table of contents, reviewing the index, and skimming a portion of the text.
- *Reputable publisher.*   University, academic, or trade presses publish most of the books you will use, which generally ensures their credibility. In addition, publishers often specialize in books related to specialized subjects.
- *Publication date.*   For many topics, sources older than ten or fifteen years have limited value. However, consider creating a historical context by using older sources.

- *Respected periodicals.* Generally, use journals with strong organizational affiliations; furthermore, peer-reviewed journals (those that publish works only after they have been recommended by a panel of expert reviewers) offer more credibility than non-peer-reviewed journals. Choose specialized, rather than general-interest, magazines. Choose major newspapers for topics of international or national importance, but choose regional or local newspapers for issues of regional or local importance.

- *Useful supplementary materials.* Look for in-text illustrations, tables, charts, graphs, diagrams, bibliographies, case studies, or collections of additional readings.

- *Appropriate writing style.* Skim a potential source to see how it is developed (with examples, facts, narration, description); also consider whether the author's style is varied, lively, and interesting.

AUDIOVISUAL SOURCES

Because of the range of audiovisual sources, assess each kind individually using individual criteria. Many of the techniques for evaluating these sources correspond to those for print and Internet sources.

- *Lectures and speeches.* Use criteria similar to those for print sources: speaker, relationship to your topic, coverage, sponsoring group or organization, and date.

- *Works of art, photographs, cartoons, and recordings.* Because these sources are used primarily to create interest in most researched papers, consider how well the image or performance illuminates the topic.

- *Maps, graphs, tables, and charts.* Evaluate these visual sources as you would traditional print sources.

- *Film, television, and radio.* When these sources serve informative purposes, evaluate them as you would print sources; when they are used creatively, evaluate them as you would art and other creative audiovisual forms.

INTERNET SOURCES

Although Internet sources provide a fascinating array of materials, much of what is posted on the Internet has not been subjected to scholarly review and is, therefore, not always credible. As a result, you should use only those Internet sources that meet important evaluative criteria:

- *Author, editor, host, or Web master's credentials.* A Web site may or may not have an author, editor, host, or Web master. If it does, explore the site for information about his or her qualifications to discuss the topic.

- *Appropriate focus.* Skim the Web site to see whether its focus is suitable for your topic. Sometimes the Web site's title makes the focus clear; at other times, an entire Web site has a general focus, but its internal links allow you to locate material on narrower aspects of the larger subject.

- *Sufficient coverage.* Review documents in the Web site to see whether the coverage is thorough enough for your purposes.

- *Domains.* Examine the Web site's electronic address (URL) to see how the site is registered with the Internet Corporation for Assigned Names and Numbers (ICANN). The following common "top-level domains" provide useful clues about a Web site's focus and function:

.com	A commercial site. The primary function of a commercial site is to make money.
.edu	A site affiliated with an educational institution.
.gov	A government site. These sites present trustworthy information (statistics, facts, reports) and less useful interpretive materials.
.mil	A military site. The technical information on these sites is consistently useful, but interpretive material tends to justify a single, pro-military position.
.museum	A site for a museum. Because museums can be either nonprofit or for-profit institutions, consider the purpose that the particular museum serves.
.org	An organizational site. Because organizations seek to advance political, social, financial, educational, and other specific agendas, review these materials with care.

- *Possible biases.* Do not automatically discount or overvalue what you find on any particular kind of Web site. Rather, consider the biases that influence how the information on a site is presented and interpreted.

- *Affiliation or sponsorship.* Examine the site to see whether it has an affiliation or a sponsorship beyond what is suggested by the site's domain.
- *Posting or revision date.* Identify the date of original posting or the date on which information was updated. Since currency is one of the benefits of Internet sources, look for sites that provide recent information.
- *Documentation.* Review Internet materials to see how thoroughly authors have documented their information. If facts, statistics, and other aspects of technical information are not documented appropriately, the information may be questionable as well.
- *Links to or from other sites.* Consider the "referral quality" that Internet links provide.
- *Appropriate writing style.* Skim the Web site to see how it is written. All sources do not, of course, have to be written in the same style, but it is an issue worth considering when you evaluate a source.

COMBINATIONS OF SOURCES

Although you must first evaluate your sources individually—whether they are print, audiovisual, or Internet—your goal is to gather a set of high-quality sources that together provide a balanced treatment of your topic. Consider these issues:

- *Alternative perspectives.* Taken collectively, does the work of your authors provide a range of perspectives—academic and popular, liberal and conservative, theoretical and practical, current and traditional?
- *Varied publication, release, or distribution dates.* Does your group of sources represent the information, ideas, and interpretations of different periods?
- *Different approaches to the topic.* In combination, your sources should range from the technical (including facts and statistics) to the interpretive (providing commentary and assessments). Also consider literature reviews for secondary analyses and empirical studies for primary research.
- *Diversity of sources.* Incorporate in your work a wide range of sources—books, periodicals, audiovisual sources, and electronic sources—to ensure that you have taken advantage of the strengths of each kind of source. Be aware, however, that in some instances your research must focus on selected kinds of sources.

Evaluating sources is an inexact process. No matter how carefully you review materials, some later prove unhelpful. Yet early efforts to evaluate sources generally make later, more comprehensive work, such as reading and taking notes from the sources, more clearly focused and productive than it otherwise would be.

1f Note-Taking

Note-taking is a personal process because different researchers prefer different methods for recording information and ideas from sources. However, all note-taking should be meticulous and consistent, both to avoid plagiarism and to simplify the subsequent writing of the paper. Consider alternative methods for note-taking and remember that note-taking must be complete, consistent, matched to the kind of material being used, and honest.

METHODS OF NOTE-TAKING

Before beginning your note-taking, analyze each note-taking system and choose the one most compatible with your specific project, library facilities, work habits, and instructor's expectations.

- *Note cards.* Note cards are easy to handle and to rearrange during planning stages, but they hold only limited amounts of information.
- *Paper.* Paper is easy to handle and has sufficient room for copious notes, but notes on paper are difficult to organize during planning stages.
- *Computers.* Notes on computers do not have to be retyped during the writing process and can be printed multiple times, but on-site note-taking with computers is sometimes awkward.
- *Photocopies and printed texts.* Photocopied and printed materials do not have to be recopied, and they can be marked on. However, photocopying and printing can be expensive.

COMPLETE INFORMATION

Record complete identifying information with each separate note to avoid having to return to a source at a later, and potentially less convenient, time.

- *Author's name.* Record the author's last name (and initial, if necessary for clarity); for multiauthor sources, record only as many names as are necessary for clarity.
- *Title.* Record only key words from titles but use italics or quotation marks as appropriate.
- *Category notation.* Provide a brief descriptive term to indicate the idea or subtopic that the information supports.
- *Page numbers.* Record the page number(s) from which you gathered information. If material comes from several pages, indicate where the page break occurs. (A double slash [//] is a useful way to indicate a page break.)

CONSISTENT FORMAT

Record notes in a consistent format to avoid confusion at later stages of research and writing.

- *Placement of information.* Establish a consistent pattern for placing information so that nothing is omitted accidentally.
- *Abbreviations.* Use abbreviations selectively to save time and space; however, use only standard abbreviations to avoid possible confusion later.
- *Notations.* Note anything unique about the source (for example, no page numbers in a pamphlet or an especially good chart).

KINDS OF NOTES

Four common kinds of notes serve most research purposes. Choose among these kinds of note-taking patterns depending on the sources you use and the kinds of materials they include.

- *Facts.* A fact note records technical information—names, dates, percentages—in minimal form. Record words, phrases, and information in a simple outline or list format and double-check the information for accuracy.
- *Summaries.* A summary note presents the substance of a passage in condensed form. After reading original material carefully, write a summary without looking at the original; this will ensure that the phrasing is yours, not

the author's. Double-check the summary note to make sure that your wording is distinct from the original.

- *Paraphrases.* A paraphrase note restates the ideas from a passage in your own words, using approximately the same number of words. Write a paraphrase without looking at the original, and then double-check the note to ensure that the phrasing is yours.

- *Quotations.* A quotation note reproduces a writer's work exactly. Double-check the quotation note against the original; the copy must be an exact transcription of the original wording, capitalization, punctuation, and other elements.

1g Plagiarism

Plagiarism, from the Latin word for *kidnapping,* is the use of someone else's words, ideas, or line of thought without acknowledgment. In its most extreme form, plagiarism involves submitting someone else's completed work as your own; a less extreme but equally unacceptable form involves copying and pasting entire segments of another writer's work into your own writing; and a third form involves carelessly or inadvertently blending elements (words, phrases, ideas) of a writer's work into your own.

- *Whole-paper plagiarism.* This kind of plagiarism is easily discovered because instructors, through experiences with students in class, learn what students are interested in and how they express themselves (sentence patterns, diction, and technical fluency).

- *Copy-and-paste plagiarism.* This kind of plagiarism is also easy to detect because of the abrupt shifts in sentence sophistication, diction, and technical fluency.

- *Careless plagiarism.* This form of plagiarism is evident when distinct material is unquoted or when specialized information (dates, percentages, and other facts) is not acknowledged. Even when this is carelessly or inadvertently done, the writer is still at fault for dishonest work, and the paper is still unacceptable.

In all its forms, plagiarism is academically dishonest and unacceptable, and the penalties for its practice range from failing individual papers or projects to failing courses to being dismissed from college to having degrees revoked. The seriousness of plagiarism cannot be ignored, so you must make a concerted effort to avoid this practice. To avoid plagiarizing, learn to recognize distinctive content and expression in source materials and take accurate, carefully punctuated and documented notes.

COMMON KNOWLEDGE

Some kinds of information—facts and interpretations— are known by many people and are consequently described as **common knowledge.** That J. Robert Oppenheimer directed the Manhattan Project is widely known, as is the more interpretative information that the development of the atomic bomb began without a clear understanding of its political impact. But common knowledge extends beyond these very general types of information to more specific information within a field of study. In studies in art, for example, it is a widely known fact that "Whistler's Mother" is the popular name for *Arrangement in Grey and Black: The Artist's Mother;* in education, a commonly acknowledged interpretation is that high scores on standardized tests do not uniformly predict academic success. Documenting these facts, beliefs, and interpretations in a paper would be unnecessary because they are commonly known in their areas of study, even though you might have discovered them for the first time.

When you are researching an unfamiliar subject, distinguishing common knowledge that does not require documentation from special knowledge that does require documentation is sometimes difficult. The following guidelines may help.

What constitutes common knowledge

- *Historical facts* (names, dates, and general interpretations) that appear in many general reference books. For example, Sigmund Freud's most influential work, *The Interpretation of Dreams,* was published in 1899.

- *General observations and opinions* that are shared by many people. For example, it is a general observation that children learn by actively doing, not passively listening, and it is a commonly held opinion that reading, writing, and arithmetic are the basic skills to be learned by an elementary school child.

- *Unacknowledged information* that appears in multiple sources. For example, it is common knowledge that the earth's population is roughly 6.5 billion people and that an *IQ* is a gauge of intelligence determined by a person's knowledge in relation to his or her age.

If a piece of information does not meet these guidelines or if you are uncertain about whether it is common knowledge, always document the material.

SPECIAL QUALITIES OF SOURCE MATERIALS

A more difficult problem than identifying common knowledge involves using an author's words and ideas improperly. Improper use often results from careless summarizing and paraphrasing. To use source materials without plagiarizing, learn to recognize their distinctive qualities:

- *Distinctive prose style.* The author's choices of words, phrases, and sentence patterns
- *Original facts.* The result of the author's personal research
- *Personal interpretations of information.* The author's individual evaluation of his or her information
- *Original ideas.* Those ideas that are unique to the particular author

As you work with sources, be aware of these distinguishing qualities and make certain that you do not appropriate the prose (word choices and sentence structures), original research, interpretations, or ideas of others without giving proper credit.

Consider, for example, the following paragraphs from Joyce Appleby, Lynn Hunt, and Margaret Jacob's *Telling the Truth about History* (New York: Norton, 1994):

> Interest in this new research in social history can be partly explained by the personal backgrounds of the cohort of historians who undertook the task of writing history from the bottom up. They entered higher education with the post-Sputnik expansion of the 1950s and 1960s, when the number of new Ph.D.s in history nearly quadrupled. Since many of them were children and grandchildren of immigrants, they had a personal incentive for turning the writing of their dissertations

into a movement of memory recovery. Others were black or female and similarly prompted to find ways to make the historically inarticulate speak. While the number of male Ph.D.s in history ebbed and flowed with the vicissitudes of the job market, the number of new female Ph.D.s in history steadily increased from 11 percent (29) in 1950 to 13 percent (137) in 1970 and finally to 37 percent (192) in 1989.

Although ethnicity is harder to locate in the records, the GI Bill was clearly effective in bringing the children of working-class families into the middle-class educational mainstream. This was the thin end of a democratizing wedge prying open higher education in the United States. Never before had so many people in any society earned so many higher degrees. Important as their numbers were, the change in perspective these academics brought to their disciplines has made the qualitative changes even more impressive. Suddenly graduate students with strange, unpronounceable surnames, with Brooklyn accents and different skin colors, appeared in the venerable ivy-colored buildings that epitomized elite schooling.

Now look at the following examples of faulty and acceptable summaries and paraphrases; questionable phrases in the faulty samples are underlined.

Faulty summary: plagiarism likely

Appleby, Hunt, Jacob   historians' backgrounds

-- A historian's focus is _partially explained_ by his or her _personal background_.

-- Because of their experiences, _they have a personal incentive_ for looking at history in new ways.

-- Large numbers were important, but the change in viewpoint _made the qualitative changes even more impressive_.

pp. 146–147

Acceptable summary: plagiarism unlikely

> Appleby, Hunt, Jacob   historians' backgrounds
>
> -- A historian's focus and interpretations are personal.
>
> -- For personal reasons, not always stated, people examine the facts of history from different perspectives.
>
> -- Large numbers were important, but the change in viewpoint "made the qualitative changes even more impressive."
>
> pp. 146–147

Faulty paraphrase: plagiarism likely

> Appleby, Hunt, Jacob   the GI Bill
>
> -- _Even though ethnic background is not easily found in the_ statistics, the GI Bill consistently helped students from _low-income families enter the middle-class educational system_. This was how _democracy started forcing open college education in America_.
>
> pp. 146–147

Acceptable paraphrase: plagiarism unlikely

> Appleby, Hunt, Jacob   the GI Bill
>
> -- Because of the GI Bill, even poor people could attend college. For the first time, education was accessible to everyone, which is truly democracy in action. The GI Bill was "the thin end of a democratizing wedge prying open higher education."
>
> pp. 146–147

1h Planning

After gathering information, organizing the research paper is an exciting stage because you are ready to bring ideas together in a clear and logical form.

REVIEWING NOTES

Begin by rereading the assignment sheet to reexamine the principles guiding your work. Then review your notes. Though time consuming, rereading all of your notes allows you to see the range of materials and connections among ideas.

THESIS STATEMENT OR STATED OBJECTIVE

After rereading your notes, revise the thesis statement, hypothesis, or objective so that it accurately represents the paper you plan to write. Is the topic clear? Does it express your current (more informed) view? Does it contain appropriate qualifications and limitations? Is it worded effectively?

AN INFORMAL OUTLINE

An informal outline is a structural plan prepared for your own use. Arrange information in logical ways using numbers, arrows, dashes, dots, or other convenient symbols to indicate the order for presentation and the relative importance of ideas.

Using the major headings from the informal outline, sort your notes. If a note fits into more than one group, place it in the most appropriate group and place a cross-reference note (for example, "See Parker quotation, p. 219—in *Childhood*") in each of the other appropriate groups.

A FORMAL OUTLINE

If you choose to develop a formal outline, adhere to the following conventions to establish divisions within the outline:

- *Major topics.* Use uppercase roman numerals (*I, II, III*) to indicate major topics.
- *Subdivisions.* Use uppercase letters (*A, B, C*) to indicate subdivisions of the major topics.

- *Clarifications.*   Use arabic numerals (*1, 2, 3*) to indicate clarifications of subdivisions—usually examples, supporting facts, and so on.
- *Details.*   Use lowercase letters (*a, b, c*) with a closing parenthesis to indicate details used to describe the examples.

> I. Major topics use capital roman numerals.
>   A. Subdivisions of major topics use capital letters.
>   1. Clarifications use arabic numerals.
>   a) Details use lowercase letters and a closing parenthesis.

In addition, observe the following conventions:

- Use parallel form throughout. Use words and phrases to develop a topic outline or use full sentences to develop a sentence outline.
- Include only one idea in each entry. Subdivide entries that contain two or more ideas.
- Include at least two entries at each sublevel.
- Indent headings of the same level the same number of spaces from the margin.

1i Writing Strategies

Because incorporating research materials and introducing reference notes extend the time it takes to write a paper, allow ample time to write the draft of your paper. Consider both the general and special circumstances that affect the process of writing and revising any paper, as well as those issues that relate specifically to writing and revising a research paper.

GENERAL STRATEGIES FOR DRAFTING A PAPER

Because the research paper is in many ways like all other papers, keep these overall writing strategies in mind:

- *Gather materials.*   Collect planning materials and writing supplies before you begin writing. Working consistently in the same location is also helpful because all materials are there when you wish to write.

- *Work from an outline.* Following an outline, develop paragraphs and sections; write troublesome sections late in the process.
- *Keep the paper's purpose in mind.* Arrange and develop only the ideas that your outline indicates are important.
- *Develop the paper "promised" by the thesis, hypothesis, or objective.* Incorporate only those ideas and information that support your thesis, hypothesis, or objective.
- *Attend to technical matters later.* Concentrate on getting your ideas down on paper; you can revise the paper later to correct any technical errors.
- *Rethink troublesome sections.* When sections are difficult to write, reconsider their importance or means of development. Revise the outline if necessary.
- *Reread as you write.* Reread early sections as you write to maintain a consistent tone and style.
- *Write alternative sections.* Write several versions of troublesome sections and then choose the best one.
- *Take a periodic break.* Get away from your work for short periods so that you can maintain a fresh perspective and attain objectivity.

STRATEGIES FOR DRAFTING A RESEARCH PAPER

Because the research paper has its own peculiarities and demands, keep these special strategies in mind:

- *Allow ample time.* Give yourself plenty of time to write a research paper; its length and complexity will affect the speed at which you work.
- *Think about sections, not paragraphs.* Think of the paper in terms of sections, not paragraphs. Large sections will probably contain several paragraphs.
- *Use transitions.* Although headings can divide your work into logical segments, use well-chosen transitional words to signal major shifts between elements of the paper.
- *Attend to technical language.* Define technical terms carefully to clarify ideas.
- *Incorporate notes smoothly.* Use research materials to support and illustrate, not dominate, your discussion.

- *Document carefully.* Use endnotes or footnotes to acknowledge the sources of your ideas and information (see Chapter 4, "Preparing Endnotes, Footnotes, and the Bibliography").

QUESTIONS FOR REVISING CONTENT

Examine the paper's content for clarity, coherence, and completeness. Consider these issues:

- *Title, introduction, headings, conclusion.* Are your title, introduction, headings, and conclusion well matched to the tone and purpose of the paper?
- *Thesis (hypothesis) and development.* Does the thesis accurately represent your current view on the topic, and does the paper develop that idea?
- *Support for thesis.* Do research materials effectively support the paper's thesis? Have you eliminated material (details, sentences, even paragraphs) that does not directly support your thesis?
- *Organization.* Does your organizational pattern present your ideas logically and effectively?
- *Use of materials.* Have you incorporated a range of materials to develop your ideas in a varied, interesting, and complete way?
- *Balance among sections.* Are the sections of the paper balanced in length and emphasis?
- *Balance in sources.* Have you used a variety of sources to support your ideas?
- *Transitions.* Do transitions connect sections of the paper in a coherent way?

QUESTIONS FOR REVISING STYLE

Achieving coherent, balanced, well-developed content is one aspect of revision. Another consideration is achieving a clear and compelling presentation. Refine the paper's style, keeping these issues in mind:

- *Tone.* Is the tone suited to the topic and presentation?
- *Sentences.* Are the sentences varied in both length and type? Have you written active, rather than passive, sentences?
- *Diction.* Are the word choices vivid, accurate, and suitable?

- *Introduction of research materials.* Have you introduced research materials (facts, summaries, paraphrases, and quotations) with variety and clarity?

Technical revision focuses on grammar, punctuation, mechanics, spelling, and manuscript form. After revising content and style, consider technical revisions to make the presentation correct and precise, giving particular attention to issues related to documentation:

- *Grammar.* Are your sentences complete? Do nouns agree with pronouns and subjects with verbs? Have you worked to avoid errors that you commonly make?
- *Punctuation and mechanics.* Have you double-checked your punctuation? Have you spell-checked the paper? Have you used quotation marks and italics accurately?
- *Quotations.* Are quotations presented correctly, depending on their length or emphasis?
- *Endnotes or Footnotes.* Are endnotes or footnotes placed appropriately and punctuated accurately?
- *Bibliography.* Is your list alphabetized correctly? Is each entry complete and correct?
- *Manuscript guidelines.* Are margins, line spacing, and paging correct? Does the paper include all necessary elements?

2 Preparing Chicago-Style Manuscripts

2a Parts of the Manuscript

TITLE PAGE

A manuscript prepared in Chicago style begins with a separate title page (see page 111 for a sample), composed of the following elements:

- *School name.* Include the full name of your college or university.
- *Paper title.* Include the title of your paper, including subtitles. If the title extends beyond one line, divide it so that the lines are of approximately equal length.
- *Course title.* Name the course for which you wrote the paper (identified by department and number, not by its descriptive title).
- *Date.* List the day on which the paper is submitted.
- *Author's name.* Include your name, introduced using the preposition *BY* (on the line above, not italicized).
- *Capitalization.* Fully capitalize all elements of the title page.
- *Centered information.* Center the elements of the title page between the right and left margins and the top and bottom margins.
- *Symmetrical spacing.* Make the line space between the school and title the same as the space between the date and your name; make the space between the title and the course the same as the space between the course title and your name. Visual symmetry is the goal.
- *Page numbering.* Do not include a page number on the title page, but count the title page in the page numbering for front matter if any elements are included preceding the text of the paper (see the sample on page 111).
- *A blank page.* Place a blank page after the title page, so that the print from the first page of the text does not show through to the title page. No page number appears on the blank page, but it is counted in the page numbering for front matter if any elements are included preceding the text of the paper.

Order of Elements of a Chicago-Style Paper*

- *Title page.* The opening page highlights the title of the paper, provides identifying information about the author, and clarifies the context in which the paper was written.

- *Blank page.* A blank page prevents subsequent text pages from showing through to the title page.

- *List of illustrations (figures).* The printed captions that accompany the numbered illustrations in the paper appear in this separate list.

- *List of tables.* The printed titles that accompany the numbered tables in the paper are presented in this list.

- *Text.* An informative or persuasive paper contains an introduction, body, and conclusion; it may be divided using headings that describe the main elements of the discussion.

- *Appendixes.* Appendixes provide supplementary information that supports the ideas of the paper but that is awkward to include in the paper itself.

- *Endnotes.* Arranged in the order in which references appear in the text of the paper, endnotes provide publishing information about sources used in the paper. (As an alternative, the same information in the same format can appear at the bottom of pages as footnotes.)

- *Glossary.* An alphabetically arranged list of foreign or technical terms, with translations or definitions, may be included.

- *Bibliography.* The bibliography is an alphabetical list of sources used in the paper; however, it may also include relevant sources related to the paper that are not cited. (Alternative labels include *Works Cited* and *Literature Cited.*)

---

* These are the key elements of most Chicago-style papers prepared for classes; more complex papers—like master's theses—may contain additional elements that are described in Appendix A.

When a paper contains a large number of illustrations (art, photographs, charts, maps, musical transcriptions, cartoons, and so on), include a list of illustrations.

- *Heading.* Two inches from the top of the page, type *ILLUSTRATIONS,* centered but not italicized. Three spaces below, type *Figure* (flush left) and *Page* (flush right); neither word is italicized. Two lines below, list the illustrations in the order in which they appear in the paper.

- *Format.* Type the number of the figure (illustration) and a period; after one space, type the figure caption as it appears in the paper. Captions are capitalized headline style in the list; in the text, however, captions are presented with sentence-style capitalization. After the caption, insert dot leaders (spaced periods that extend across the line) and include the number of the page on which the figure appears, flush right.

- *Vertical alignment.* To maintain symmetry, align the periods that follow figure numbers; also align the periods of dot leaders.

- *Line spacing.* Single-space elements, with double-spacing between listed items.

- *Indentation.* If the caption for a figure extends beyond one line, indent the carry-over line three to five spaces under the caption (not the figure number).

- *Page numbering.* Number a list of illustrations as front matter, using lowercase roman numerals. Counting the title page and the blank page, a list of illustrations begins on page iii. The number is centered at the bottom of the initial page of a list of illustrations; if the list requires additional pages, the page numbers appear at the top of subsequent pages.

A sample list of illustrations appears in Appendix C.

Preparing Figures

In the text of the paper, include visual elements—art, photographs, charts, maps, musical transcriptions, cartoons, and so on—according to these guidelines:

- *Placement.* Include a figure as close as possible to the textual discussion: on the same page or on the

(cont. on next page)

Preparing Figures

following page. Separate a figure from the primary text by inserting three lines above and below the figure caption.

- *Numbering.*   Number figures consecutively throughout the paper; in-text references should then be to the figure number ("See figure 4 for an example.").
- *Identifying information.*   Three lines below the figure (flush left), type the abbreviation *Fig.*, not italicized, the figure number, and the figure caption.
- *Figure captions.*   Captions are most often words or phrases that briefly describe or label a figure; however, they may also be sentences. Capitalize them sentence style and follow them with a period.
- *Credit lines.*   If you did not create the figure, include a credit line. One space after the figure caption, enclose complete citation information within parentheses. These citations are not repeated in endnotes or footnotes, but the sources are included in the bibliography.

Special Concerns for Figures

- *Value of the figure.*   Consider whether the figure presents information more effectively than would a textual discussion or a table. Because figures are more difficult to prepare than print-based elements, make sure that your time is well spent in creating one.
- *Computer-generated figures.*   Today's word-processing programs are capable of creating a wide range of figures, including bar graphs, line graphs, and pie charts. Allow sufficient time to learn to use these computer features.
- *Imported images.*   When copying and pasting images from Internet sources—versus scanning images into your document—adjust them to fit the page, being sure to maintain the aspect ratio (top-to-bottom/side-to-side proportions).
- *Visual clutter.*   Include only figures that highlight important elements of your discussion. To achieve this goal, eliminate all extraneous detail in graphs,

charts, and drawings and crop (trim) photographs and maps to focus visual attention on key features, not superficial or unrelated elements.

- *Visual clarity.* To ensure that figures achieve maximum impact, make sure that the print quality of graphs and charts is high (best achieved by laser printing). Furthermore, make sure that bar charts, photographs, art, and maps are sharply focused and have clear tonal contrast.

LIST OF TABLES

When a paper contains a large number of tables, include a list of tables.

- *Heading.* Two inches from the top of the page, type *TABLES,* centered but not italicized. Three spaces below, type *Table* (flush left) and *Page* (flush right); neither word is italicized. Two lines below, list the tables in the order in which they appear in the paper.

- *Format.* Type the number of the table and a period; after one space, type the table title as it appears in the paper. Table titles are capitalized headline style in the list; in the text, however, table titles are most frequently presented with sentence-style capitalization, although headline-style capitalization is also acceptable. After the title, insert dot leaders (spaced periods that extend across the line) and include the number of the page on which the table appears, flush right.

- *Vertical alignment.* To maintain symmetry, align the periods that follow figure numbers; also align the periods of dot leaders.

- *Line spacing.* Single-space elements, with double-spacing between listed items.

- *Indentation.* If the title of a table extends beyond one line, indent the carry-over line three to five spaces under the title (not the table number).

- *Page numbering.* Number a list of tables as front matter, using lowercase roman numerals. Continue the numbering of other front matter. The number is centered at the bottom of the initial page of a list of tables; if the list requires additional pages, the page numbers appear at the top of subsequent pages.

A sample list of tables appears in Appendix C.

Preparing Tables

In the text of the paper, include tables to present labeled information in columns (vertical separations) and rows (horizontal separations) for easy interpretation and comparison.

- *Placement.*   Include a table as close as possible to the textual discussion: on the same page or on the following page. Separate a table from the primary text by inserting three lines above and below the table. (Alternately, tables may be placed in appendixes.)

- *Numbering.*   Number tables consecutively throughout the paper; in-text references should then be to the table number ("See table 3 for the range of responses.")

- *Identifying information.*   Three lines below the text (flush left), type *Table* (not italicized) followed by the number and a period. After one space, present the table's title with either sentence-style or headline-style capitalization.

- *Horizontal ruled lines.*   Insert ruled lines below the table number, below the column headings, and below the last row of the table.

- *Column headings.*   Insert column headings, using headline-style capitalization; center the headings over the information in each column. One line below the column headings, insert a horizontal ruled line.

- *Labels for rows.*   Use words or brief phrases (called *stubs*) to label each row; use sentence-style capitalization.

- *Symmetry.*   Space columns evenly and provide the same amount of space between rows (single or double).

- *Source note.*   If you did not create the table, include a source note. Below the horizontal ruled line that closes the table, type the word *Source,* in italics, followed by a colon. After the colon, include complete citation information, followed by a period. These citations are not repeated in endnotes or footnotes, but the sources are included in the bibliography.

- *General note.* To provide clarifying information, you may also include a general note. Two spaces below either the table's closing ruled line or its source note, type the word *Note,* in italics, followed by a colon; then provide necessary details, explanations, or clarifications, followed by a period.

THE TEXT

Two inches from the top, center the title of the paper (in all capital letters); three spaces below, the text begins. This first textual page is considered page 1 in the numbering of the pages; the number appears at the bottom of the page, centered. Subsequent pages are numbered at the top of the page (either centered or flush right).

An Argumentative Paper or Review

- *Introduction.* In this unlabeled section, define, describe, or clarify the topic (problem); place it in its historical or scholarly context. Present a thesis (a statement of your topic and opinion).
- *Body.* Examine the facets of the topic (problem) by reviewing current research: evaluate the positions held by others; analyze current data; assess the interpretations of others; synthesize the information and ideas found in other people's work. If helpful, use headings and subheadings throughout this section to direct readers through your argument.
- *Conclusion.* Summarize key points, draw connections among important ideas, and reiterate your thesis.
- *Endnotes.* In this labeled section, include reference notes for individual materials used throughout the paper.
- *Bibliography.* In this labeled section, provide a list of sources cited in the paper—and, perhaps, of other relevant sources (see chapter 4).
- *Additional materials.* As appropriate, include front matter (list of illustrations and list of tables) and back matter (appendixes and glossary).

APPENDIXES

One or more appendixes may be included immediately after the text.

- *Heading.*   Two inches from the top of the page, type *APPENDIX*, centered but not italicized. If more than one appendix is included, label each one with a number or letter (*APPENDIX 1, APPENDIX 2* or *APPENDIX A, APPENDIX B*).
- *Appendix title.*   A single appendix requires no title. However, if more than one appendix is included, place its title one line below the heading, centered and in full capitals.

APPENDIX 3
TRANSCRIPT OF AN INTERVIEW WITH
FRANCISCO JIMÉNEZ

- *Text.*   Begin the appended material three lines below the appendix's heading or title. Single-spacing or double-spacing is acceptable, depending on the material.
- *Paging.*   Begin each appendix on a new page and continue the page numbering of the paper. On the opening page of each appendix, the page number is centered at the bottom; subsequent pages of each appendix are then numbered at the top, centered or flush right.

ENDNOTES

Use endnotes to list reference notes at the end of a paper, rather than at the bottom of each relevant page (footnotes). Endnotes correspond to sequential numbers in the text of the paper that indicate when ideas, information, or language has been used from other sources. Prepare an endnote page according to these guidelines.

- *Heading.*   Two inches from the top of the page, type *NOTES*, centered but not italicized. Three lines below, begin the first note.
- *Order of notes.*   Place endnotes on the notes page in the order in which references appear in the paper. Double-check the numbering.

- *Format.*   Type endnotes paragraph style, with the first line indented and subsequent lines aligned with the left margin. "Tab" once (for a five-space indentation) and insert the appropriate number and a period. After one space, add appropriate note information.
- *Spacing.*   Single-space entries, but double-space between them.
- *Paging.*   Continue the page numbering of the paper on the notes page. On the opening notes page, the page number is centered at the bottom; subsequent pages are then numbered at the top, centered or flush right.

Placing Note Numbers in the Paper

- *In-text notes.*   Notes, whether presented as endnotes or footnotes, are numbered sequentially throughout a paper.
- *Placement of note numbers.*   In the text of the paper, refer to a note by using a superscript number (a number placed above the line, like this[1]) without additional space. Word-processing programs allow you to achieve this result by using the "Font" feature.
- *Punctuation and note numbers.*   Note numbers follow all punctuation marks, except dashes and parentheses. A note number precedes the dash[2]—without additional space. A note number may appear within parentheses (when it refers only to the materials within parentheses[3]). If the note refers to the entire sentence, however, it follows the parentheses (as in this sample).[4]

GLOSSARY

When a paper includes a substantial number of foreign or technical terms, a glossary provides helpful translations or definitions without disrupting to the primary text. When helpful, prepare a glossary following these principles.

- *Heading.*   Two inches from the top of the page, type *GLOSSARY,* centered but not italicized. Three lines below, begin the first definition. (If more than one glossary is included, each should be numbered and titled.)

- *Alphabetical order.* Arrange the terms in alphabetical order.
- *Format.* Beginning at the left margin, type each term and follow it with a period or a colon. After one space, type the translation or definition; if it is expressed in sentence form, close with a period. If an entry extends more than one line, indent second and subsequent lines five spaces.
- *Spacing.* Single-space entries, but double-space between them.

A sample glossary appears in Appendix C.

BIBLIOGRAPHY

The bibliography, which continues the paging of the entire manuscript, provides publishing information for all the sources used in the paper (see page 124 for a sample). Chapter 4 provides a comprehensive discussion of the information required in bibliographic entries and the format for presenting the information. Chapters 5–8 provide explanations of 65 kinds of sources, with note entries for books and other print materials, periodicals, audiovisual sources, and electronic sources.

2b   General Manuscript Guidelines

PAPER

Use heavy-weight white bond $8^{1}/_{2} \times 11$ paper. Acid-free paper is preferred.

FONT SELECTION

Fonts—designed versions of letters, numbers, and characters—appear in different sizes, referred to as *points.* Chicago style strongly recommends the use of serif fonts (those with cross marks on individual letters). Book Antiqua, `Courier New`, Times New Roman, and other similar fonts are acceptable in either pica (12-point, a large print size) or elite (10-point, a smaller print size). Laser or ink-jet printing is preferred.

   Use italics, not underlining, within your manuscripts to identify the titles of books, periodicals, albums, paintings, and so on.

LINE SPACING

Double-space the primary text of the paper. However, single-space selected elements: footnotes, endnotes, block quotations, captions, headings that extend more than one line, sources included in the bibliography, and visual elements like tables and charts. When elements are single-spaced, separate them with two line spaces.

NOTE: The fifteenth edition of the *Manual* allows double-spacing throughout the manuscript (see *Manual* 2.12); however, to achieve the look of a finished document, block quotations, footnotes, endnotes, and bibliographic entries are often single-spaced, with double-spacing before and after.

MARGINS AND INDENTATIONS

A one-inch margin on the left side is required; a one-and-one-half-inch margin on the left is preferred; a one-inch margin is required for the bottom and the right side of the page. Do not justify the right margin; instead, leave a ragged text edge. On the first page of a paper (or section), the top margin must be two inches; on subsequent pages, a one-inch margin is required.

Indent paragraphs and notes five spaces using the "Tab" feature. Use the "Indent" feature (which establishes a continuous five-space indentation) for block quotations (those over one hundred words) and for second and subsequent lines of bibliographic entries and other special elements.

PAGING

The first page of a section—such as the first page of the text or endnotes or the bibliography—has the page number centered at the bottom. Subsequent pages within sections follow one of two styles: page numbers may be centered at the top of the page or placed in the upper right corner (so long as the style is applied consistently throughout). The numbers in either style must be at least three-quarters of an inch from the top margin.

Most word-processing programs allow you to change the position of page numbers easily, a page at a time, to accommodate these styles.

TITLES AND HEADINGS FOR SECTIONS

The title of a paper (and of special sections within the paper) is positioned two inches from the top of the page, centered and in all capital letters; a title that extends beyond one line is single-spaced, with three line spaces before the text begins.

When headings are required to divide and subdivide a paper into logical sections, follow these patterns:

- *First-level headings* are centered, in italics or bold, using headline-style capitalization.
- *Second-level headings* are centered with sentence-style capitalization; they do not use distinguishing print features.
- *Third-level headings* begin at the left margin, in italics or bold, with headline-style capitalization.
- *Fourth-level headings* begin at the left margin, are capitalized sentence style, and are presented without special print features.
- *Fifth-level headings* follow a paragraph indentation; they are in italics or bold and have sentence-style capitalization; after one space, the paragraph continues.

When new headings are required, do not begin new pages. Simply leave a three- or four-line space and type the heading. The text begins three or four line spaces below the heading.

THE TITLE OF A PAPER

First-Level Heading

Second-level heading

Third-Level Heading

Fourth-level heading

    Fifth-level heading. The paragraph continues after one space.

SUBMITTING THE PAPER

Submit manuscripts according to your instructor's guidelines. If you receive no specific guidelines, secure the pages with a paper clip in the upper left corner and place them in a manila envelope with your name and identifying information about the paper typed or written on the outside. Always keep another printed copy—or a photocopy—of the paper.

Be aware that instructors may ask for a disk copy of the paper. If they do, submit a copy of the final paper on a separate disk, clearly labeled with your name and course information, as well as a note about your word-processing program (for example, Microsoft Word 2000, Word Perfect 10). Keep a backup disk version for yourself.

ORDER OF THE MANUSCRIPT

Place your manuscript pages in this order, noting that all elements are not required:

- Title page (unnumbered)
- Blank page (unnumbered)
- List of illustrations (optional, roman numeral iii)
- List of tables (optional, continues roman numeral sequence)
- Text (begin on page 1)
- Appendix (optional, continues arabic numeral sequence)
- Endnotes (an alternative to footnotes, continues arabic numeral sequence)
- Glossary (optional, continues arabic numeral sequence)
- Bibliography (may or may not be required, continues arabic numeral sequence)

A longer or more comprehensive paper, such as a thesis or dissertation, may include additional elements (see Appendix A).

3 Following Chicago Editorial Style

3a Punctuation and Mechanics

Generally, Chicago style follows conventions that need little explanation (for example, periods follow sentences that make statements, and question marks follow sentences that pose questions). However, in some situations, agreement about editorial issues is not universal (Should commas separate all elements of listed items? Are conjunctions in titles capitalized?). In such special circumstances, follow the Chicago guidelines in this chapter to ensure that your manuscript meets expectations.

PERIODS

Periods most often serve as end punctuation (after sentences), but they are also used with abbreviations and in other specialized contexts.

Uses of periods	*Examples*
End of a complete sentence	A period is followed by one space.
Initials with an author's name	C. S. Lewis, Edward P. J. Corbett
Abbreviations in notes and bibliographies	ed., rev. ed., trans., vol.
After figure captions expressed as full sentences	Fig. 3. Funding increased between 1954 and 1964.
Latin abbreviations	i.e., e.g., vs., P.M.
To show omissions in quotations (ellipsis points: three spaced periods)	Garvey reported, "The people involved in the project . . . have a great deal at stake." (see page 65 for additional examples)
End of an endnote or footnote	1. Toni Morrison, *Beloved* (New York: Knopf, 1987), 65.

Uses of periods	*Examples*
Separate elements of a bibliography entry	Adler, Mortimer J. *Reforming Education: The Opening of the American Mind.* Ed. Geraldine Van Doren. New York: Macmillan, 1988.

COMMAS

Commas are internal forms of punctuation, most often used to separate elements within sentences. However, they also serve a few other purposes.

Uses of commas	*Examples*
Three or more items in a series	men, women, and children
Set off nonessential information	The exhibit, which had been recently installed, was in the south wing.
Clauses of a compound sentence	The first negotiation was a failure, but the second one was a success.
After an opening dependent clause	Although he was from a wealthy family, Roosevelt championed the poor.
After an opening adverbial phrase	After seven hours, the jury delivered its verdict.
Modifiers that function separately	The expansive, newly restored train station
Years with exact dates	May 25, 2006, the museum was dedicated. *But* The museum was dedicated May 2006.
To introduce a brief quotation	President Truman is known to have said, "The buck stops here."
Numbers of 1,000 or larger (every three numbers)	11,205 students, 1,934 books (see "Number Style," page 52, for exceptions)

(cont. on next page)

Uses of commas	*Examples*
With *yes, no,* interjections, or names in direct address	Yes, it is constitutional to replicate the flag for personal use. Well, you can protest if you like. Jeremy, please answer the question without editorializing.

SEMICOLONS

In Chicago style, semicolons serve two purposes, one related to compound sentences and one related to elements in a series.

Uses of semicolons	*Examples*
Join clauses of a compound sentence when no coordinating conjunction is used	Corporate donations to the presidential library were surprisingly small; private donations were surprisingly large.
Separate elements in a series when the elements contain commas	The symphony tour included performances in Washington, DC; St. Louis, Missouri; and Denver, Colorado.
Separate two references within the same note	1. Molière, *The School for Wives,* trans. Richard Wilbur (New York: Harcourt, Harvest, 1971), 2.3; William Wycherley, *The Country Wife,* ed. James Ogden (New York: Norton, 1991), 2.1.

COLONS

Colons serve five distinct purposes in Chicago style. A complete sentence must precede the colon when it introduces clarifying material. If the explanatory material that follows a colon incorporates two or more sentences, the first word of each clarifying sentence is capitalized.

Uses of colons	*Examples*
Introduce a word, phrase, or sentence that serves as an explanation or illustration	Two words triggered the strongest reactions: *preferential* and *special.* (phrase) The results are quickly summarized: the debate was a failure. (one sentence) His options were very clear: He could stay. He could go. (two sentences)
Separate a title and subtitle	Harold Bloom's *The American Religion: The Emergence of the Post-Christian Nation*
Separate the place of publication and publisher in notes and bibliographies	1. Robert Perrin, *Handbook for College Research,* 3rd ed. (Boston: Houghton Mifflin Co., 2005), 76.
Introduce a long quotation—or a quotation with special emphasis	Ernest Hemingway made this observation: "Writing is architecture, not interior design."
Separate chapter and verse in biblical references (in notes and bibliographies)	Gen. 11:1–9, Mark 10:23–25 (periods may also be used: Gen. 11.1–9)

QUESTION MARKS

Question marks are used to indicate a direct question or to indicate uncertainty; the second use should be very selective.

Use of question marks	*Examples*
Direct question	How is personal correspondence documented?
Uncertainty	In her diary, Abigail Harris (1920?–2001) described the events of the 1939 flood.

EXCLAMATION POINTS

The exclamation point (!) expresses excitement or surprise and should be used sparingly in academic writing. It should not be used to indicate an ironic observation or to imply an editorial challenge of quoted material.

HYPHENS

Hyphens serve two purposes in Chicago style. They link words that collectively modify another word: *four-phase research, ninth-grade student, word-processing program.* They also separate numbers and letters that are not inclusive: (telephone number) 1-866-436-5701, (ISBN number) 0-618-30820-2, (spelling) "Her name is spelled K-e-r-y-n."

DASHES

The en dash (slightly longer than the hyphen) is used to connect inclusive numbers or dates: 12–15, 231–33, 1955–2005 (see page 53 for a discussion of inclusive numbers). Insert the en dash from the "special characters" set of your word-processing program.

The em dash is the most commonly used dash. It can be inserted from the "special characters" set of your word-processing program, or it can be formed by typing two hyphens. Either way, no spaces should separate the em dash from the words before and after. In academic writing, dashes should be used selectively.

A 3-em dash (which can be typed as three em dashes or six hyphens) is used in bibliographies to indicate a repeated name.

Uses of dashes	*Examples*
Indicate a break in the thought of the sentence	The national heritage of participants—they identified themselves—proved less important than we anticipated.
Insert a series of elements that contain commas	Universities in two small cities—Terre Haute, Indiana, and Bloomington, Illinois—offer similar degree programs in psychology.

Uses of dashes	*Examples*
Indicate a repeated author in a bibliography: a 3-em dash	Havel, Václav. *Disturbing the Peace.* Trans. Paul Wilson. New York: Knopf, 1990.
	———. *Letters to Olga: June 1979–September 1982.* Trans. Paul Wilson. New York: Holt, 1990.

PARENTHESES

Parentheses are used—always in pairs—to separate information and elements from the rest of the sentence.

Uses of parentheses	*Examples*
Set off clarifying information	Four versions of the manuscript exist (see figures 1–4).
Introduce an abbreviation to be used in place of a full name in subsequent sections of a paper	The American Library Association (ALA) hosts its annual conference in the spring. Graduate students attend ALA meetings in ever-increasing numbers.
Set off numbers or letters that indicate divisions or sequences	The test included sections on (1) vocabulary, (2) reading comprehension, (3) inferences, and (4) error identification.
Set off publication information in an endnote or footnote	2. Ernest L. Boyer, *College: The Undergraduate Experience in America* (New York: Harper, 1987), 13.

To indicate the fourth level of a formal outline (closing parenthesis only)	I. Major topics
	    A. Subdivisions
	        1. Clarifications
	            a) Details

BRACKETS

Brackets are used within parentheses or quotation marks to provide clarifying information. Use brackets sparingly because they can become distracting in academic writing.

Uses of brackets	*Examples*
Parenthetical information already in parentheses	(See figure 4 [Percentages of students with learning disabilities] for more detailed information.)
Clarifying information in a quotation	Thompson observed, "When [students] work in groups, they are more comfortable and perform better."[1]
Phonetic transcriptions	The Greek dramatic term *deus ex machina* [da′es eks mä′k e-nä] describes extraordinary and artificial means to resolve an issue or problem.

SLASHES

Slashes serve very specialized functions, often related to the presentation of alternatives or compounds.

Uses of slashes	*Examples*
Alternatives	first-day/second-day experiences
Fractions (numerator/denominator)	3/4, X + Y/Z
Indicate phonemes in English	/b/
Lines of poetry in a paragraph (with spaces before and after)	"In Xanadu did Kubla Khan / A stately pleasure dome decree."[2]
Multiple publication dates	2. John Palmer, *The Comedy of Manners* (London: Bell, 1913/1962), ix.

QUOTATION MARKS

Quotation marks are used within the body of a paper to identify titles of some works, to indicate a quotation containing fewer than one hundred words (or roughly eight lines of text), and to highlight words used in special ways.

Periods, commas, and parentheses precede the closing quotation mark; colons and semicolons follow the closing quotation mark. Question marks precede the closing quotation mark if the quotation is a question; question marks follow the closing quotation mark if the entire sentence is a question.

In those instances when quotation marks are needed within already quoted material—for example, a song title within an article title—the internal marks appear in single form.

Uses of quotation marks	*Examples*
Titles of chapters, articles, songs, subsites of Web sites, and so on	"Pandering in Politics" (chapter), "Grant Writing v. Grant Getting" (article), "My Vietnam" (song), "Great American Speeches" (subsite)
Quoted material (written or spoken) of fewer than one hundred words when used word for word	Rodriguez observed, "There are things so deeply personal that they can be revealed only to strangers."[3]
Words used counter to their intended meaning (irony, slang, or coined usage)	Her "abnormal" behavior was, in fact, quite normal.
Titles within titles (single within double)	"Pieces of 'Pied Beauty' "

ELLIPSIS POINTS

Ellipsis points are made by typing three spaced periods. If ellipsis points are inserted between sentences, retain the punctuation of the remaining sentences.

Uses of ellipsis points	*Examples*
To show omissions in quotations	Harrison observed, "The best management qualities . . . can be found in our entrepre-neurial businesses; the worst are in government."[4]
To indicate a pause or a break in thought	I considered the proposal . . . and then considered it again.

CAPITALIZATION

In Chicago style, the universally accepted practice of cap-italizing the first word of sentences and capitalizing proper or specific names causes few problems. Other specific patterns are discussed below.

Titles of elements of papers—headings, figure cap-tions, table titles, and so on—may appear in one of two basic styles: sentence style and headline style.

Sentence-Style Capitalization

Guiding principles	*Examples*
Capitalize the first word of a title or subtitle; otherwise, capitalize only proper nouns and proper adjectives.	Fig. 1. Survey of property owned by Thomas Jefferson; Table 1. Published material, arranged by archive; Jefferson's commitment to university education (level-four heading)

Headline-Style Capitalization

Guiding principles	*Examples*
Capitalize the first and last word; capitalize all other words except articles, prepositions of any length, *to* (as part of an infinitive phrase), and conjunctions of fewer than four letters	*The Chicago Manual of Style;* "First Ladies and Public Engagement: The Legacy of Eleanor Roosevelt"; *Critical Theory since Plato;* To Commit, to Defend, to Abandon (level-two heading)

Uses of capitalization	*Examples*
Proper nouns and proper adjectives	Bruce Catton, Zora Neale Hurston, Chinese students, Elizabethan architecture
Titles and epithets (nicknames)	Secretary of State Kissinger, the Reverend Martin Luther King Jr., the Great Communicator, the Little Tramp
Titles of works (excluding articles, prepositions, *to* [as part of an infinitive phrase], and conjunctions of fewer than four letters)	*Journal of the Plague Year,* "Battle Hymn of the Republic," *All the President's Men,* "To Know You Is Not Necessarily to Love You"
Historical events, movements, and periods	the Middle Ages, the French Revolution, the Boston Tea Party, the Great Depression
Specific place names and regions	Jakarta, South Africa, Vermont, Midwest (but midwestern), the Beltway
Specific departments (and academic units) in universities and specific courses	Department of History, Indiana State University, African American Studies 336
Trade and brand names	Prozac, Xerox, WordPerfect 10
Specific titles for parts of books	"Jazz and the American Sensibility" (but chapter 4)
Ethnic names (not involving color)	Caucasians, Latinos, Seminoles, Vietnamese
Headings that divide a text (both sentence and headline styles)	**First-Level Heading,** Second-level heading, *Third-Level Heading,* Fourth-level heading
Titles of papers and major subsections (all capitals)	READING, WRITING, AND RESIGNATION: VICTORIAN WOMEN'S EDUCATION; APPENDIX A; NOTES; BIBLIOGRAPHY

(cont. on next page)

Uses of capitalization	*Examples*
Specific calendar names	Wednesday, April (but fall, winter)
Web sites (headline style)	The Victorian Web, Smithsonian Education

Special cases— No capitalization	*Examples*
General references to departments and courses	a number of departments of music, an art history course
General names	president, professor, college, association
General names of laws or theories	the empirical law of effect
Standard parts of books, plays, or other print materials	chapter 16, scene 1, column 2, row 6
Titles of poems known by first lines (capitalize only what the poet capitalized)	Shakespeare's "When, in disgrace with Fortune and men's eyes"

ITALICS

Chicago recommends the use of italics (*slanted fonts,* as in this example), rather than underlining, in computer-generated manuscripts.

When an italicized title contains an element that should itself be italicized, present the embedded element without italics: *Social Construction in Wharton's* House of Mirth: *Status, Class, and Conventions.*

Uses of italics	*Examples*
Titles of full-length works: books, periodicals, films, albums, and so on	*The Unheavenly City* (book), *American Scholar* (periodical), *The New World* (film), *Born in the USA* (album)

Uses of italics	*Examples*
Works of art	Hopper's *Ryder's House;* Ruscha's *Standard Oil Station, Amarillo, Texas;* Picasso's *Guernica*
Musical works with assigned or attributed names (but not by form, key, or number)	Dvořák's *From the New World,* Copland's *Appalachian Spring;* but Symphony no. 9, Cello Suite No. 1 in G Major
Legal cases	*Brown v. Board of Education* [Little Rock]
New terms (introduced and defined)	The term *Nisei,* meaning second-generation Japanese Americans
Words, letters, or phrases used as words, letters, or phrases	Different impressions are created by the words *small, diminutive, minute,* and *tiny.*
Words that could be misread	more *specific* detail (meaning additional detail that is specific)
Letters used as symbols or algebraic variables	$IQ = \dfrac{MA \text{ (mental age)}}{CA \text{ (chronological age)}} \times 100$
Unfamiliar foreign words	Forming a stage picture— a *mise en scène*—requires a sense of visual balance.
Headings (some, not all)	*Third-Level Heading, Fifth-level heading*
Ships and aircraft	the *Titanic, Queen Elizabeth II, Air Force One,* the *Spruce Goose*
Rhyme schemes (with unspaced commas to indicate stanza breaks)	*abab, cdcd, efef, gg*

NUMBER STYLE

In Chicago style, spelled-out numbers are used more frequently than numerals, whether in written texts or supporting materials. Arabic numerals are used most often; roman numerals are reserved for the paging of front matter (vii), for numbers with names (Charles II), and for designations for sequels *(The Godfather II),* and for major divisions of a formal outline (see page 20).

Uses of words for numbers	*Examples*
Numbers through one hundred (see exceptions in the following table)	two senatorial campaigns, three engravings, a six-minute song
Whole numbers larger than one hundred	four thousand, six million
Numbers that begin sentences	One hundred forty citizens attended the town meeting.
Numbers that represent currency (used with the word *dollars*)	six dollars, two hundred sixty dollars
Numbers that represent decades or centuries (Alternative: see "Uses of numerals")	the twenties, the sixties, the eighteenth century, nineteenth-century art
Numbers that begin titles	"Twelve Common Errors in Research," *Seven-Point Scales: Values and Limitations*
Numbers that begin headings	Five common income groups (table heading)
Numbers in common fractions	two-thirds of teachers, a three-fourths reduction
Numbers in common names and phrases	the Seven Deadly Sins, the Ten Commandments, the Seven Wonders of the World
Numbers to indicate whole hours	three o'clock in the evening, eleven o'clock in the morning

Uses of numerals	*Examples*
Numbers to mark a sequence or series (in parentheses)	Follow these steps: (1) gather your sources, (2) create bibliographic entries, and (3) take notes.
Numbers in comparison	the 4th chapter of 20; 2 of 10 archeological sites; 15 sources: 3 books, 10 articles, 1 film, and 1 interview
Numbers used in addresses	1600 Pennsylvania Avenue, 10 Downing Street
Names with (roman) numerals to indicate family order	Henry IV, Queen Elizabeth II, Marcus Fitzgerald III
Numbers used statistically or mathematically	7.5 of respondents, a ratio of 5:2, the 3rd percentile, multiplied by 3
Numbers that indicate percentages	either 17% or 17 percent
Numbers that represent exact times or whole hours used with A.M. or P.M.	8:45 in the morning, 6:15 P.M., 9:00 A.M.
Numbers that represent dates	April 1, 2005; November 2006
Numbers that represent decades (Alternative: see "Uses of words for numbers")	1880s, 1920s, 1960s
Numbers that refer to points or scores on a scale	scores of 6.5 on an 8-point scale
Numbers for exact sums of money (used with $)	The cost of the booklet was $4.25.
Whole numbers combined with fractions	$8^1/_2 \times 11$ inches, $5^1/_4 \times 7^1/_4$ feet
Numbers used as numbers	a scale ranging from *1* to *10*

(cont. on next page)

Uses of numerals	*Examples*
Numbers that indicate placement in a series	exam 4, figure 9
Numbers for parts of a work	chapter 2, page 6, scene 3, stanza 4
References to the Bible, classical, or medieval works	Gen. 1:13–16, *Iliad* 1.6.13

To indicate the first level of a formal outline	I. Major topics
	  A. Subdivisions
	    1. Clarifications
	      a) Details

Cardinal and Ordinal Numbers

Cardinal numbers (*one, two, three,* and so on) indicate quantity; ordinal numbers (*first, second, third,* and so on) indicate order. The principles described in the preceding tables apply, whether the numbers are cardinal or ordinal.

Commas in Numbers

In most writing contexts, commas are used in numbers of 1,000 or larger. Place commas between groups of three digits, moving from the right. However, commas are not used in page references.

Numbers without commas	*Examples*
Page numbers	page 1287, pages 1002–21
Numbers that function as units: addresses, serial numbers, years, and so on	2256 Ohio Boulevard (address), 033776901 (serial number), 1998 (year)

Plurals of Numbers

Whether numbers are presented as numerals or words, form their plurals by adding only *s* or *es.* Do not use apostrophes to indicate plurality: 1960s, threes, 25s.

Inclusive Numbers

Inclusive numbers indicate the beginning and ending of a number sequence: page ranges for chapters or other parts of works, page locations for extended quotations or materials that are summarized, or ranges in dates. Chicago style allows for the change of only the new element (2002–3, 189–91, 15–7) or the repetition of all elements (2002–2003, 189–191, 15–17); however, the preferred Chicago style is described in the table below. Use an en dash (from the "special features" of your word-processing program) between the numbers.

Inclusive Numbers		
Number range	**General rule**	*Examples*
1–100	Use all numbers	5–25, 40–46, 93–100
101–9 (201–9, and so on)	Include only the changed number	102–3, 407, 605–7
110–199 (210–99, and so on)	Include at least two digits	111–17, 358–74, 993–99
Any three-digit change (of a four-digit number)	Use all four numbers	1699–1743, 2369–2401

3b General Style

The way in which a manuscript is written affects the ways in which readers respond. A well-written paper communicates ideas efficiently and effectively, whereas a poorly written paper distracts readers from its central ideas. Consequently, take time to revise your writing to improve its presentation, especially considering a few key elements that improve the effectiveness of communication.

TRANSITIONS

Transitions—words or phrases that signal relationships among elements of a paper—facilitate readers' progress

through a paper. Use transitions to create appropriate
links within your work (see box below).

Transitional Words and Phrases

Relationship	*Examples*
Addition	also, and, besides, equally, further, furthermore, in addition, moreover, next, too
Similarity	also, likewise, moreover, similarly
Difference	but, however, in contrast, nevertheless, on the contrary, on the other hand, yet
Examples	for example, for instance, in fact, specifically, to illustrate
Restatements	finally, in brief, in conclusion, in other words, in short, in summary, on the whole, that is, therefore, to sum up
Results	accordingly, as a result, consequently, for this reason, so, therefore, thereupon, thus
Chronology	after, afterward, before, during, earlier, finally, first, immediately, in the meantime, later, meanwhile, next, second, simultaneously, soon, still, then, third, when, while
Location	above, below, beyond, farther, here, nearby, opposite, there, to the left, to the right, under

---

VERB TENSE

Verbs are primary communicators in sentences, signaling
action *(organize, summarize, present)* or indicating a
state of being *(seem, was)*. Well-chosen, specific verbs
make writing direct and forceful. Moreover, tenses of
verbs indicate chronology, clarifying the time relationships that you want to express.

In Chicago style, verbs are used in specific ways to signal ideas clearly.

Uses of verbs	*Examples*
Active voice (to clarify who is doing what)	Archivists have cataloged and stored documents over the last two decades. (Archivists are emphasized.)
Passive voice (to clarify who or what received the action, not the person or people responsible)	Over the last two decades, documents have been carefully cataloged and carefully stored. (The documents are emphasized, not the unacknowledged archivists.)
Past tense (to place an action in the past or to describe previous research)	Bradshaw and Hines summarized their research in one incisive paragraph.
Present perfect tense (to describe an action that began in the past and continues to the present)	In the years since, researchers have incorporated Piaget's methods in a variety of studies of children.
Subjunctive mood (to describe a conditional situation or one contrary to fact)	If the records were complete, our analysis would be less conjectural.

AGREEMENT

Agreement is the matching of words or word forms according to number (singular and plural) and gender (masculine, feminine, or neuter). Verbs take singular or plural forms depending on whether their subjects are singular or plural. Pronouns must match their antecedents (the words to which they refer) in both number and gender.

Subject–Verb Agreement

Special Circumstances | *Examples*

Foreign words—*datum* (singular) versus *data* (plural), *phenomenon* (singular) versus *phenomena* (plural), and others: choose the correct form.

The data suggest that our preconceptions were ill founded. (plural subject/plural verb) The phenomenon is unlikely to occur again. (singular subject/singular verb)

Collective (or group) nouns: consider whether members of the group act in unison (singular) or individually (plural).

Congress approves appropriations each fiscal year. (singular meaning to stress shared action) The research team interview Holocaust survivors. (plural meaning to stress individual action by many members)

Singular and plural subjects joined by *or* or *nor:* match the verb to the nearer subject.

Neither the panelists nor the moderator finds the facility acceptable. *Or:* Neither the moderator nor the panelists find the facility acceptable

Pronoun–Antecedent Agreement

Special Circumstances | *Examples*

Agreement in number: Match the pronoun to its antecedent. (Also see "Biased Language," pages 59–61.)

At commencement, a doctoral student receives his or her diploma and hood. singular) At commencement, doctoral students receive their diplomas and hoods. (plural)

Agreement in gender: Match the pronoun to the antecedent. (Also see "Biased Language.")

Devon was the first student to complete his exam. (masculine)

Special Circumstances	Examples
Who and *whom:* Use *who* in a subject position; use *whom* in an object position.	Who is responsible for compiling the data? (subject: He or she is.) To whom should we address our inquiries? (object: Address it to him or her.)

PARALLELISM

Parallelism is the use of equivalent forms when words are used together: nouns, verbs of the same tense or form, and so on.

Special Circumstances	Examples
Elements in a series: Use matching forms.	Even young children are expected to add, to subtract, and to multiply. (parallel verb forms) Reading, writing, speaking, listening, and thinking compose the language arts. (parallel gerund/ noun forms)
Correlative conjunctions (*both/and, either/or, neither/nor, not only/ but also*): Use matching forms of the words, phrases, and clauses that are linked.	The youngest child in a large family is either the most independent or the least independent of the siblings. (parallel phrases) We found not only that the experiment was too costly but also that it was too time consuming. (parallel clauses)

3c   Word Choice

Word choice makes meaning clear to readers. Specific word choices affect the tone of writing—implying your perception of yourself, your readers, your subject, and your purpose in writing. Consequently, choose words carefully to communicate ideas effectively.

NOUN CLUSTERS

Noun clusters are created when nouns, often in multiples, are used to modify yet another noun. Although the modification patterns may be grammatically correct (nouns *can* function as modifiers), they often create dense clusters of meaning that have to be sorted through carefully. For example, the phrase *field research funding initiative* is long, does not read smoothly, and has to be deconstructed. To improve readability, untangle the nouns and place them in easily readable phrases: *an initiative to fund field research.* The reconstructed phrase is easier to interpret than the original and, therefore, communicates the idea more efficiently than does the original.

JARGON

Jargon is the specialized language of a professional group. In some instances, a specific technical term communicates an idea more efficiently than an explanation in everyday language. For instance, the phrase *correlational analyses* explains in two generally understood words a process by which data are both systematically linked and logically compared. However, in many instances, common language that is well selected communicates ideas in a more straightforward and less pretentious way. For example, in many instances the phrase *classroom teacher* communicates an idea with greater clarity and less distraction than the more affected phrase *teacher/practitioner,* which is a stilted way of expressing an idea that is implicit in the word *teacher.*

In your writing, choose words with care. Use technical jargon only when it communicates ideas clearly and efficiently—that is, when it is precise and helpful. Never use jargon to impress because an overreliance on technical terms (especially those that do not communicate ideas precisely and quickly) frustrates readers and clutters prose.

COLLOQUIALISMS

In academic writing, avoid colloquialisms, expressions that are better suited for conversation and other forms of informal communication. Words and phrases such as *write-up* (instead of *report*), *only a few* (rather than *10 percent*), or *get-together* (in place of *meeting* or *colloquium*) not only lack the specificity of more technical, formal language but also suggest a lack of precision that may make readers question the care with which you have completed your research. For these reasons, use precise, professional language in your writing.

SPECIFICITY

Choose specific words to create clear meaning; do not assume that readers will infer meaning from vague language. For example, rather than writing that a survey contained "numerous questions," be specific and indicate that it contained seventy-five questions. Instead of noting that recommendations were based on the responses "of many historians," describe the group more precisely: one hundred scholars at doctoral-granting institutions. Even this description could be made more specific by noting the numbers of male/female respondents (if that would prove helpful), the kinds of schools (public, private), the locations of the schools (by state or region), and other variables.

The credibility of research depends on using language that communicates clearly. Consequently, choose words that are as specific as possible.

BIASED LANGUAGE

Whether employed consciously or unconsciously, biased language conveys a writer's insensitivity, ignorance, or, in some instances, prejudice—any of which disrupts communication because readers expect to find balance and fairness in what they read. Writing that incorporates biased language reflects badly on the writer, alienates thoughtful readers, and consequently interferes with effective communication.

As a writer, you should make a concerted effort to use accurate, equitable language. Recognizing that your potential readers represent a broad spectrum of society, choose words with care and avoid stereotypes.

Racial and Ethnic Bias

Language that is racially and ethnically biased often relies on dated words related to racial or ethnic groups. In other instances, racially and ethnically biased word choices ignore the distinct groups that exist within larger classifications, thereby perpetuating broad stereotypes.

Consequently, it is preferable to refer to racial or ethnic groups as specifically as possible (see table below).

Preferred Racial or Ethnic Terms		
Questionable	Preferred terms for American citizens	Preferred terms for non-American citizens
Arab	Arab American; or Saudi American, Iraqi American, Afghan American, and so on	Saudi, Iraqi, Afghan, and so on
Hispanic	Latino/Latina, Chicano/Chicana; or Mexican American, Cuban American, and so on	Mexican, Cuban, Costa Rican, and so on
Indian	Native American; or Cherokee, Ogallala Sioux, Seminole, and so on	Mesoamerican, Inuit, and so on
Black	African American; or Kenyan American, Ugandan American, and so on	African; or Ugandan, Kenyan, and so on
White	European American; or Italian American, French American, Irish American, and so on	Caucasian, European; or German, French, Hungarian, Russian, and so on
Oriental	Asian American; or Japanese American, Korean American, Chinese American, and so on	Asian; or Korean, Japanese, Vietnamese, and so on

Gender Bias

Language based on stereotypical gender roles—also called sexist language—implies through choices of nouns, pronouns, and adjectives that people fall into preassigned roles. Because gender-biased language fails to reflect the diversity of contemporary society, it is inaccurate. Replace nouns that imply gender exclusivity—for example, *chairman* or *spokesman*—with words whose gender-meanings are neutral (*chairperson* or *spokesperson*).

Avoid using gender-specific pronouns when their antecedents are not gender specific. The most common concern is the generic use of a masculine pronoun *(he, him, his, himself)* as in this sentence: "A lawyer is bound by professional oath to keep his clients' records confidential." Although this usage was once acceptable, today's writers and readers expect pronoun use to be inclusive, not exclusionary. Solutions include using alternate pronouns ("A lawyer is bound by professional oath to keep his or her clients' records confidential."), plural forms ("Lawyers are bound by professional oath to keep their clients' records confidential."), and omission of the pronoun when no confusion is likely ("A lawyer is bound by professional oath to keep clients' records confidential.").

Avoid using gender-related adjectives when other modifiers create similar meaning without bias or when gender is not an issue: "The male administrative assistant was both competent and friendly" is better presented this way: "The administrative assistant was both competent and friendly."

Other Forms of Bias

Be sensitive to the ways in which your language characterizes people by age, class, religion, region, physical and mental ability, or sexual orientation. Do your word choices create stereotypical impressions that disrupt your discussions? Do they convey unintended but negative feelings? Will they offend potential readers and therefore distract them from your ideas? Examine your writing carefully for instances of these kinds of bias and explore alternative ways to convey your meaning.

4 Preparing Endnotes, Footnotes, and the Bibliography

Requiring endnotes (listed at the end of the paper) or footnotes (placed at the "foot," or bottom, of individual pages), Chicago style provides full publication information within each notation. Because notes in Chicago style are thorough, you can frequently omit a bibliography; at other times, instructors require one.

This chapter includes detailed discussions of the information required for and the formatting of notes; chapters 5–8 provide explanations and examples of the most commonly used sources for Chicago-style papers. In addition, the book includes some sources that are not traditionally used in professional writing but that are potentially useful for students' writing; the principles of Chicago-style documentation have been applied in preparing these samples.

4a Endnotes and Footnotes — An Overview

Note numbers in the paper indicate when writers use materials from other sources; these in-text numbers correspond to either endnotes or footnotes. Both kinds of notes contain the same information, presented in the same format. They vary only in their placement in relation to the text of the paper: endnotes are listed after the paper, whereas footnotes appear at the bottom (or "foot") of the page. Either style is acceptable, but some institutions, departments, and instructors prefer one to the other. You should, therefore, determine which format to use in your specific context.

4b Placing Note Numbers in the Paper

At the end of a phrase, sentence, paragraph, or other element containing or referring to information from a source, place a note number one-half space (not a full space) above the line. Use the "Superscript" feature (one of the options within the "Font" feature) of your word-processing program to place numbers above the line automatically.

Placing Note Numbers

- *Sequential numbers.* Notes are numbered sequentially throughout a paper.
- *Placement.* In the text of the paper, refer to a note by using a superscript number (one-half space above the line, like this[1]) without additional space.
- *Punctuation and note numbers.* Note numbers follow all punctuation marks, except dashes and parentheses. A note number precedes the dash[2] — without additional space. A note number may appear within parentheses (when it refers only to the material within parentheses[3]). If the note refers to the entire sentence, however, it follows the parentheses (as in this sample).[4]

Use only one note per sentence to avoid confusion; however, single notes may include references to multiple sources (see page 67).

4c Information for Endnotes and Footnotes

Endnotes and footnotes vary only in their location in relation to the text; otherwise, they present information in identical fashion. They must follow an established order for presenting information. To combine forms (to list a translation of a second edition, for example), use these guidelines to determine the order in which to include information.

1. *Authors and editors.* Take the name or names from the title page of a book or the first page of an article. Authors' names are listed in the order in which they appear, which may or may not be alphabetical. Do not include professional titles or degrees, even though they may be listed. If no author (individual or organization) is listed, the note begins with the title.

2. *Title.* List full titles, including subtitles, taking information from the title page of a book or from the first page of an article.

3. *Additional information.* Include any of the following information *in the order presented here* if it is listed

on the title page of the book or on the first page of an article, essay, chapter, or other subsection:

- editor
- compiler
- translator
- edition number
- volume number
- name of series

4. *Facts of publication.* Locate facts of publication on the title page and copyright page (immediately following the title page). List the first city (place of publication) if more than one is given. If needed for clarity, include an abbreviation for the state, province, or country, using either two-letter postal abbreviations or Chicago-style abbreviations (see Appendix B). You can shorten a publisher's name or use it in full form, so long as you are consistent throughout your notes and bibliographic entries (see box below). In either style, exclude the article *The* and corporate designations *(Company, Limited, Incorporated);* however, retain the word *Books* (and *Press* if it is associated with a university). When *University* is part of the publisher's name, it may be abbreviated *(Univ.)* if the pattern is applied consistently in all notes and bibliographic entries. Use the most recent publication date shown. For periodicals, take the volume number, issue number, and date from the masthead (the listing of information found at the top of the first page of a newspaper or within the first few pages of a journal or magazine, often in combination with the table of contents).

5. *Page numbers.* Include the page number or numbers from which you gathered ideas, information, or quotations (see page 53 for guidelines for presenting inclusive numbers).

Shortened Forms of Publishers' Names		
Drop given names or initials	Harry N. Abrams	Abrams
Use the first of multiple names	Farrar, Straus, and Giroux	Farrar

Shortened Forms of Publishers' Names		
Drop corporation designations	Doubleday and Co., Inc.	Doubleday
Use standard abbreviations	Government Printing Office	GPO

4d Format for Endnotes and Footnotes

To ensure easy reading, notes must follow this format consistently:

- *Indentation patterns.* Indent the first line of each note five spaces (one "Tab"). Begin the note with an arabic number and a period; after one space, include full note information. Subsequent lines begin at the normal left margin. As an alternative, you can use superscript note numbers (one-half space above the line), followed by the first element of the note; in this format, no space should separate the note number from the first letter of the first word.

- *Authors' names.* List authors' names in complete form and normal order *(Jean Paul Sartre, Edmund Morris).*

- *Authorless sources.* When no author is named, begin the note with the source's title.

- *Titles.* Use the complete title, no matter how long; a colon and a space separate the title from the subtitle. Titles appear with headline-style capitalization and italics or quotation marks, as appropriate. You may regularize type styles—that is, convert a title presented in lowercase into headline-style capitalization or use the word *and* instead of an ampersand (&).

- *Punctuation within entries.* Separate major sections of entries (author, title, publication information, and pages) with commas. When a title ends with a question mark or an exclamation point, retain the comma. Enclose facts of publication—city, publisher, and date—in parentheses, followed by a comma and page reference.

- *Line spacing.* Single-space the notes themselves, but double-space between them.

4e Positioning Endnotes and Footnotes

Endnotes are listed in a separately titled section at the
end of the paper; a full discussion of how to prepare that
section appears in chapter 2 (see pages 32–33).
Footnotes, which provide information at the "foot," or
bottom, of the text page on which a reference occurs, require special treatment.

Most word-processing programs have a footnoting
feature that automatically places notes at the bottom of
the page and formats the notes according to generally accepted patterns. Two lines below the text of the paper, a
two-inch line separates the text from the footnotes. Two
lines below this separation line, begin the single-spaced
footnote (following the guidelines noted above). When
more than one note appears at the bottom of the page,
separate the notes with two spaces (see pages 133–135).

4f Multiple Notes from
the Same Source

When citing a source multiple times in a paper, you do
not have to repeat full information. Instead, the first note
reference to a source must provide full information; subsequent references can be shortened, as long as clarity is
maintained.

THE SAME SOURCE — CONSECUTIVE NOTES

If two references to the same source and the same page
appear without an intervening note, *ibid.,* the abbreviation for *ibidem* (Latin for "in the same place"), may be
used in the second note; it is not italicized.

    1. Laurence Rees, *Auschwitz: A New History* (New York:
Public Affairs, 2005), 16.
    2. Ibid.

If consecutive notes are to the same source but to a
different page, *ibid.* may also be used; however, the new
page number must be added. Notice that the period for
the abbreviation *ibid.* is followed by a comma.

    3. Ibid., 23.

THE SAME SOURCE—NONCONSECUTIVE NOTES

When notes to the same source do not appear consecutively, *ibid.* is not used. Instead, use the author's last name (to refer readers to the earlier note), followed by a comma and the page reference. To distinguish between two sources by the same author, include a shortened form of the title; to distinguish between two authors with the same last name, include first names as well.

> 4. Thomas, 17.
> 5. Thomas, *Myths,* 78.
> 6. Clayton Thomas, 135.

4g Multiple References in the Same Note

Although writers should not assign more than one note number to a single sentence, it is possible to provide several source references within a single note. Place the note number within the text; in the note, present information for each source, separated by semicolons. The sources can be arranged chronologically or in the order in which references appear in the text.

> 7. Telhain Shibley, *The Stakes: America in the Middle East: The Consequences of Power and the Choice of Peace* (Boulder, CO: Westview, 2004), 118; James R. Vaughn, *The Failure of American and British Propaganda in the Arab Middle East, 1945–57: Unconquerable Minds* (New York: MacMillan, Palgrave, 2005), 42.

4h The Bibliography—An Overview

The bibliography is an alphabetical list of sources used in the paper; however, it may also include relevant sources related to the paper that are not cited. (Alternative labels include *Works Cited* and *Literature Cited.*)

4i Information for Bibliographic Entries

Although the formatting is different, entries for a Chicago-style bibliography contain the same information that appears in the endnotes or footnotes. In a few instances—when authors use pseudonyms, when sources have four or more authors—bibliographic entries contain more information.

Because Chicago-style notes are so thorough, many instructors do not require corresponding bibliographies. When a bibliography is required, however, you can develop the entries by reformatting the notes and arranging them in alphabetical order.

4j   Format for Bibliographic Entries

To ensure easy reading, entries for a bibliography must follow these guidelines:

- *Indentation patterns.* Begin the first line at the left margin; subsequent lines are indented five spaces. Use the "Indent" feature of your word-processing program to ensure a continuous indentation.
- *Alphabetical order.* The entire list is arranged in alphabetical order.
- *Authors' names.* Invert initial author's names *(Sartre, Jean Paul; Morris, Edmund)* and arrange all sources in alphabetical order. Second and subsequent authors' names are in normal order, since they are not alphabetized. Multiple works by the same author are treated distinctly (see page 70).
- *Authorless sources.* Authorless works are alphabetized by their titles, excluding the articles *a, an,* and *the.*
- *Punctuation with entries.* Separate elements of a bibliographic entry with periods. When other end punctuation is used (for example, when a title ends with a question mark), the period may be omitted.
- *Line spacing.* Single-space the entries themselves, but double-space between them.

4k   Alphabetizing the Bibliography

The bibliography must be in alphabetical order, which seems simple enough. Reality often proves more complicated, however, so follow the guidelines in the box on page 69.

Circumstances	Rule and sample
Letter-by-letter style (up to a comma)	Alphabetize one letter at a time: *Jonson, Aaron L.* precedes *Jonson, David; Our American Heritage* comes before *Our American Legacy*
Spaces between words	Unless separated by commas, ignore spaces between words: *New Deal* precedes *Newhouse,* which comes before *New Therapies*
Initials instead of names	Alphabetize names with initials before spelled-out names with the same letters: *Abernathy, T.* precedes *Abernathy, Teresa.*
Names with prepositions	Follow the preference of the individual: *Beauvoir, Simone de* precedes *de Gaulle, Charles,* which precedes *Du Bois, W. E. B.*
Multiple works by the same author	Multiple works by the same author may be arranged alphabetically by title: E. D. Hirsch Jr.'s *Cultural Literacy: What Every American Needs to Know* precedes his *The Philosophy of Composition;* the works can also be arranged chronologically by publication date.
Single-author and multiple-author works	Single-author works precede multiple-author works: *Kelly, Marjorie* precedes *Kelly, Marjorie, and Hunter Fitzgerald.* Note: invert only the name of the first author.
Groups, institutions, or organizations as authors	Use the form identified with the source—either acronym or spelled-out name; alphabetize accordingly.
Authorless works	Alphabetize authorless works by title, excluding the articles *a, an,* or *the:* "The Will of the People" precedes "A Year's Worth of Budget Cuts."

41   Specialized Elements of a Bibliography

Given its special purpose and arrangement of elements, a bibliography requires, in a few special instances, patterns that vary slightly from those of either endnotes or footnotes.

DISTINCT ELEMENTS IN BIBLIOGRAPHIES

Multiple Works by Same Author

When citing multiple works by the same author, the first entry uses the author's name (in last name-first name order). A 3-em dash (which can be typed as three em dashes or six hyphens) indicates the repeated name in subsequent entries. Single-author works precede co-authored works.

Ehrenreich, Barbara. "Barefoot, Pregnant, and Ready to
     Fight." *Time,* May 8, 2002, 62.
———. "Looking to Put Fatherhood in Its Proper Place." *New
     York Times,* June 20, 1999, late ed., L14.
———. "Who Needs Men? Addressing the Prospect of a
     Matrilinear Millennium." Interview. With Lionel Tiger.
     Harper's, June 199, 33–46.
Ehrenreich, Barbara, Elizabeth Hess, and Gloria Jacobs. *Re-
     Making Love: The Feminization of Sex.* Garden City,
     NY: Doubleday, Anchor, 1986.

Four or More Authors or Editors

Although a reference note includes only the name of the first author, plus the abbreviation *et al.* ("and others"), a bibliographic entry includes up to ten names. Otherwise, the entry shares the same information as an endnote or footnote.

Tucker, Susan Martin, Mary M. Canobbio, Eleanor Vargo
     Paquette, and Margorie Fyfe Wells. *Patient Care
     Standards: Collaborative Planning and Nursing
     Interventions.* 8th ed. St. Louis: Mosby-Yearbook, 2004.

Authors Using Pseudonyms

Although a reference note includes only the pseudonym under which a selection was published, the bibliographic entry places the author's real name in brackets.

Seuss, Dr. [Theodore Seuss Geisel]. *Horton Hears a Who!*
     New York: Random, 1954.

ANNOTATED BIBLIOGRAPHIES

An annotated bibliography follows the pattern of a traditional bibliography but adds brief commentary on or evaluations of each source. After completing the normal bibliographic entry, follow one of two patterns:

- *Continuous style.* One space after the entry's closing period, add your annotation while maintaining the indentation pattern of the bibliography entry.
- *Paragraph style.* Double-space after an entry, indent five spaces, and insert the annotation (returning to the normal margin with subsequent lines).

Continuous style

Graham, Katharine. *Personal History.* New York: Knopf, 1997. *Personal History* is a detailed and interesting account of the life of a woman born into a privileged and powerful family. It is fascinating, in part, because of her sense of commitment and purpose as it extends from her personal life to her work as owner and publisher of the *Washington Post* during the Watergate era.

Paragraph style

Graham, Katharine. *Personal History.* New York: Knopf, 1997.

   Personal History is a detailed and interesting account of the life of a woman born into a privileged and powerful family. It is fascinating, in part, because of her sense of commitment and purpose as it extends from her personal life to her work as owner and publisher of the *Washington Post* during the Watergate era.

4m   Quotations

When an author's manner of expression is unique or when his or her ideas or language are difficult to paraphrase or summarize, quote the passage in your text. To avoid plagiarism, quoted material must be reproduced word for word—including exact spelling and punctuation—and must be properly separated from your text and accurately documented.

Some Verbs Used to Introduce Quotations			
add	declare	offer	restate
answer	emphasize	reiterate	say
claim	explain	remark	stress
comment	note	reply	suggest
conclude	observe	respond	summarize

BRIEF PROSE QUOTATIONS (FEWER THAN ONE HUNDRED WORDS)

A quotation of fewer than one hundred words (approximately eight lines of text) appears within a normal paragraph, with the author's words enclosed in quotation marks and marked with a superscript note number.

> Czeslaw Milosz observes, "Even if it takes Christian and humane forms, religiously oriented nationalism threatens to abolish a clear distinction between what is due God and what is due Caesar. Yet Caesar means not necessarily the rulers of the state; Caesar can also mean the society at large and a collective pressure."[1] His concerns, though directed toward contemporary Poland, apply in many national contexts.

Note form

1. Czeslaw Milosz, "On Nationalism," in *Beginning with My Streets: Essays and Recollections*, trans. Madeline G. Levine (New York: Farrar, 1991), 89.

BRIEF VERSE QUOTATIONS (ONE OR TWO LINES)

Include verse quotations of one or two lines within the paragraph text. Use quotation marks, indicate line divisions with a slash (/) preceded and followed by one space, and retain the poem's capitalization.

> In "Morning at the Window," T. S. Eliot offers a familiar and foggy image, the distant musings of a person who observes life but does not seem to live it: "The brown waves of fog toss up to me / Twisted faces from the bottom of the street."[2]

Note form

    2. T. S. Eliot, "Morning at the Window," in *The Complete Poems and Plays: 1909–1950* (New York: Harcourt, 1971), 16.

LONG PROSE QUOTATIONS (ONE HUNDRED WORDS OR MORE)

A quotation of one hundred words (approximately eight lines) or more is set off from the primary text. Known as a "block quotation," the lengthy quoted material is indented five spaces, is single-spaced, and appears without quotation marks. Retain quotation marks that appear in the original text and paragraph indentations if more than one paragraph is quoted.

Joseph W. Alsop's leisurely, charming observations on Washington, DC, during the 1930s create an impression of a place quite unlike the Capital City today:

> In that old summer Washington, before the days of daylight saving time, it was possible to dine outdoors coolly and comfortably when the night air came down the Potomac River valley after sundown. The river, itself, was so free of pollution that people quite regularly swam in it. Radio was a curiosity and television unknown, so one could think, talk, and, indeed, work in relative serenity. Only the very rich owned motor cars, but trolleys were plentiful, and, if one was in a hurry, there were also plenty of taxis. Nor were there any suburbs to speak of, so that a trip to the country was still, in those days, a bona fide and welcome retreat.[3]

Clearly, much has changed in the nation's most important political city.

Note form

    3. Joseph W. Alsop, "Dining-Out Washington," in *Katharine Graham's Washington* (New York: Vintage, 2002), 139.

LONG VERSE QUOTATIONS (THREE OR MORE LINES)

To quote three or more lines of poetry, follow the pattern for long prose quotations: indent five spaces, single-space the lines, and omit quotation marks. Using the five-space indentation as the starting point, follow the poet's indentation patterns as closely as possible.

> In "Poem [1]," Langston Hughes offers a spare, critical assessment of western culture:
>> I am afraid of this civilization —
>>> So hard,
>>>> So strong,
>>>>> So cold.[4]

In only twelve words, Hughes provides a sharp, insightful observation about the world around him.

Note form

> 4. Langston Hughes, "Poem [1]," in *The Collected Poems of Langston Hughes,* ed. Arnold Rampersad and David Roessel (New York: Knopf, 1994), 116.

PUNCTUATION WITH QUOTATIONS

Single Quotation Marks. To indicate an author's use of quotation marks within a brief quotation (which is set off by double quotation marks), change the source's punctuation to single quotation marks, as in this example:

> T. Kue Young stressed the cautionary and even alarmist nature of current approaches to healthcare management. He asserted, "Each year as many as 40,000 to 50,000 articles are published where the term *risk* appears in the titles and abstracts—this has lead some observers to refer to a 'risk epidemic' in the medical literature."[5]

Note form

> 5. T. Kue Young, *Population Health: Concepts and Methods,* 2nd ed. (New York: Oxford University Press, 2005), 177.

Because long block quotations do not begin and end with quotation marks, the source's quotation marks remain double, as in this example:

James Sellers suggests that self-identity is often inextricably linked to an individual's nationality:

> The United States is the "oldest new nation," we are often told by political scientists; and the national heritage, while it has certainly not turned out to be a "melting pot," has become a powerful background influence upon the identity of Americans, reshaping even the ways in which they express their ethnicity or religion.[6]

Whatever our race, religion, or ethnicity are, we are, perhaps most obviously, Americans.

Note form

6. James Sellers, *Essays in American Ethics* (New York: Lang, 1994), 97.

Brackets. Use brackets to indicate that you have either added words for clarity or introduced a substitution within a quotation. Most often, the words you add are specific nouns to substitute for pronouns that are vague outside the context of the original work. However, you may substitute a different tense of the same verb (for example, *used* for *use*).

In analyzing the problem-solving skills of creative people, Sheila Henderson observed: "[Inventors] recalled the freedom they were given to explore their surrounding environments and the tolerance their parents and educators showed if they made a mess, broke something, or shorted out electrical circuits as a result of their inventive endeavors."[7] Such forbearance from adults, Henderson's study suggested, is integral to developing creative problem-solving skills.

[Changed: Henderson's original phrase—*The participants*—lacks specificity outside its original context.]

Note form

7. Sheila J. Henderson, "Inventors: The Ordinary Genius Next Door," in *Creativity: From Potential to Realization,* ed. Robert J. Sternberg, Elena L. Grigorenko, and Jerome L. Singer (Washington, DC: American Psychological Association, 2004), 119.

Ellipsis points.   Use ellipsis points—three spaced periods—to indicate where words have been omitted within a quotation. To indicate an omission at the beginning or end of a sentence, retain the sentence's punctuation (producing four spaced periods).

> William Miller observed that socially constructed self-esteem is inextricably tied to other people's praise: "Flattery is narcotic and addicting. It preys on two desperate and inescapable desires: to be thought well of by others and to think well of ourselves. . . . They are complexly intertwined."[8]

[Omitted: "The second desire depends on the first more than the first on the second; in any event,"]

Note form

8. William Miller, *Faking It* (Cambridge: Cambridge University Press, 2003), 96.

5 Preparing Note Forms for Books and Other Separately Published Materials

Note Forms for Books and Other Separately Published Materials

5a A Book by One Author
5b A Book by Two or Three Authors
5c A Book by Four or More Authors
5d A Book with No Author Named
5e A Book by an Author Using a Pseudonym
5f A Book with an Organization as Author
5g An Edition Other than the First
5h A Revised or Enlarged Edition
5i A Reprinted Book
5j A Multivolume Work
5k An Edited Collection
5l A Selection in an Edited Collection
5m Multiple References to the Same Collection
5n An Article in an Encyclopedia or Other Reference Work
5o A Work in a Series
5p An Imprint
5q A Translation
5r A Government Document — *Congressional Record*
5s A Government Document — Committee, Commission, Department
5t A Preface, Introduction, Foreword, Epilogue, or Afterword
5u A Pamphlet or Brochure
5v Published Proceedings from a Conference
5w A Dissertation
5x A Book Written in a Language Other than English
5y Sacred Writings
5z A Secondary Source

Books provide comprehensive, extended discussions of topics. Those published by scholarly or university presses are often targeted to specialists in particular fields and provide a broad range of technical information and complex analyses. Those published by trade (commercial) publishers often are directed to nonspecialists.

Because books take several years to produce, they often provide reflective interpretations that have the benefit of critical distance. Consequently, they provide balance in research. To prepare reference notes for books, follow the guidelines in this chapter.

5a   A Book by One Author

A note for a single-author book begins with his or her name, followed by the title of the book, facts of publication (in parentheses), and a page reference. Book titles are capitalized headline style and italicized.

    1. Milada Anna Vachudová, *Europe Undivided: Democracy, Leverage, and Integration after Communism* (New York: Oxford University Press, 2005), 292.

    2. Thomas Goodrich, *The Darkest Dawn: Lincoln, Booth, and the Great American Tragedy* (Bloomington: Indiana University Press, 2005), 176.

5b   A Book by Two or Three Authors

When a book has two or three authors, list their names in the order presented on the title page, which may or may not be alphabetical order. Other elements of a reference note are the same as for a single-author book.

    1. John Downing and Charles Hubbard, *Representing "Race": Racisms, Ethnicities, and Media* (Thousand Oaks, CA: Sage, 2005), 211.

    2. Fred Anderson and Andrew Cayton, *The Dominion of War: Empire and Liberty in North America, 1500–2000* (New York: Viking, 2005), 109.

5c   A Book by Four or More Authors

When a book has four or more authors, list only the first author's name, followed by e*t al.,* the abbreviation for *et alii.* (Latin for "and others"); alternately, you can use the descriptive phrase *and others* (not italicized). When you are required to include a separate bibliography for your paper, include all authors' names (see page 70).

1. Susan Martin Tucker et al., *Patient Care Standards: Collaborative Planning and Nursing Interventions,* 7th ed. (St. Louis: Mosby-Yearbook, 2000), 448.

2. Edward L. Gershey and others, *Low-Level Radioactive Waste: From Cradle to Grave* (New York: Van Nostrand, 1990), 174.

5d   A Book with No Author Named

When no author is named, list the book by title. If an "authorless" book has been edited, you can list the book by editor to emphasize his or her work. Use the same emphasis both in reference notes and in corresponding bibliographic entries.

1. *An Anglo-Saxon Chronicle,* ed. M. J. Swanton (Exeter, England: University of Exeter Press, 1990), 34.

This note emphasizes the work itself.

2. M. J. Swanton, ed., *An Anglo-Saxon Chronicle* (Exeter, England: University of Exeter Press, 1990), 34.

3. *The Associated Press Stylebook and Briefing on Media Law,* ed. Norm Goldstein (New York: Perseus Books, 2002), 41.

5e   A Book by an Author Using a Pseudonym

Use the pseudonym only; if a bibliography is included with the paper, that entry includes the author's real name within brackets (see page 70).

1. George Eliot, *The Journals of George Eliot,* ed. Margaret Harris and Judith Johnson (New York: Cambridge University Press, 1998), 118–21.

2. Dr. Seuss, *Horton Hears a Who!* (New York: Random, 1954), 16–17.

5f   A Book with an Organization as Author

When an organization is both the author and the publisher, spell out the name completely in both the author and publisher positions.

1. American Psychological Association, *Publication Manual of the American Psychological Association,* 5th ed. (Washington, DC: American Psychological Association, 2001), 15–22.

5g   An Edition Other than the First

The edition number, noted on the title page, follows the title of the book; however, when a book also has an editor, translator, or compiler, the edition number follows that information. Edition numbers are presented in abbreviated form (2nd ed., 3rd ed., 4th ed.), not spelled out.

> 1. *Forging the American Character: Readings in United States History,* ed. John R. M. Wilson, 4th ed. (Upper Saddle River, NJ: Prentice, 2003), 83.
> 2. *The Psychology of Gender,* ed. Alice H. Eagly, Anne E. Ball, and Robert J. Sternberg, 2nd ed. (New York: Guilford, 2004), 319.

5h   A Revised or Enlarged Edition

Place abbreviated information about revised or enlarged editions after the title.

> 1. Martin P. Wattenburg, *The Decline of American Political Parties: 1952–1996,* enlarged ed. (Cambridge, MA: Harvard University Press, 1998), 83.
> 2. Earnest Nagel, James R. Newman, and Douglas R. Hofstadter, *Gödel's Proof,* rev. ed. (New York: New York University Press, 2002), 84.

5i   A Reprinted Book

To refer to a reprint, a newly printed but unaltered version of a book, list original facts of publication first, followed by the information about the reprint. Add a note to clarify your use of page references.

> 1. John Palmer, *The Comedy of Manners* (London: Bell, 1913; repr., New York: Russell, 1962), 288–89. Citations are to the reprinted edition.

5j   A Multivolume Work

To refer to an entire multivolume set, present the collection by its complete title, followed by the total number of volumes and the facts of publication.

2. *American Men and Women of Science,* ed. Pamela M. Kalte and Katherine H. Nenen, 21st ed., 8 vols. (Detroit: Gale, 2003).

To emphasize a single volume, include the volume number after its title, followed by the facts of publication.

2. J. M. Roberts, *The Age of Revolution,* vol. 7, *The Illustrated History of the World* (New York: Oxford University Press, 1999), 23–24.

5k   An Edited Collection

Edited collections can be listed either by title or by editor. A reference to a complete volume does not include a page reference.

1. *Against the Wall: Israel's Barrier to Peace,* ed. Michael Sorkin (New York: New Press, 2005).

OR

1. Michael Sorkin, ed., *Against the Wall: Israel's Barrier to Peace* (New York: New Press, 2005).

5l   A Selection in an Edited Collection

Author, selection title (in quotations), and collection title (italicized) are followed by the editor's name; after the editor's name, list the inclusive pages for the selection, followed by the facts of publication and page reference.

1. J. Bruce Jacobs, "'Taiwanization' in Taiwan's Politics," in *Cultural, Ethnic, and Political Nationalism in Contemporary Taiwan,* ed. John Makeham and A-Chin Hsaiu, 17–54 (New York: Palgrave, 2005), 21.

2. Diana J. Reynolds, "The Great Exhibition of 1851," in *Events That Changed Great Britain since 1689,* ed. Frank W. Thackeray and John E. Findling, 98–111 (Westport, CT: Greenwood, 2002), 109.

Chicago-style notes for collections do not distinguish between original or reprinted selections. To emphasize an original publication, include a statement at the end of the bibliography entry.

5m   Multiple References to the Same Collection

When multiple references come from the same collection (multiple essays, articles, chapters, poems, and so on), you can avoid unnecessary repetition by cross-referencing the first note in which publication information appears.

    1. Rizal Sukma, "Indonesia's Perceptions of China: The Domestic Bases of Persistent Ambiguity," in *The China Threat: Perceptions, Myths, and Reality,* ed. Herbert Yee and Ian Storey, 181–204 (London: Routledge, 2002), 199.

    5. Taeho Kim, "South Korea and a Rising China: Perceptions, Policies, and Prospects," in *The China Threat,* 166–80 (see note 1), 174.

    13. Jonathan D. Pollack, "American Perceptions of Chinese Military Power," in *The China Threat,* 43–64 (see note 1), 57.

5n   An Article in an Encyclopedia or Other Reference Work

Well-known reference books require no publication information other than the title and edition number. Less familiar reference works or recently published ones require full publication information. Include (1) the name of the reference work, (2) the edition, (3) the abbreviation *s.v.* (for *sub verso,* meaning "under the word," not italicized), and (4) the term as it appears in the reference work, in quotation marks. To emphasize the writer of the entry, include his or her name in parentheses at the end of the note.

    1. *The New Grove Dictionary of Music and Musicians,* 2001 ed., s.v. "Salieri, Antonio" (by Rudolph Angermüller).

    2. Richard M. Abrams, "Theodore Roosevelt," in *The Presidents: A Reference History,* ed. Henry F. Graff, 2nd ed. (New York: Scribner's, 1996), 331.

    The long article in this reference source is treated like a chapter from a book, and a page number is required because the articles on presidents are arranged chronologically, not alphabetically.

5o   A Work in a Series

Names of series (collections of books related to the same subject, genre, or time period) are typically found on the title page and should be included just before the publishing information, presented with headline-style capitalization. If series titles have been assigned numbers, include them after the series title, using the abbreviation *no.* (not italicized) for number.

>   1. B. J. Fogg, *Persuasive Technology: Using Computers to Change What We Think and Do,* Interactive Technology Series (Boston: Kaufman, 2003), 131.
>   2. Evelyn Waugh, *A Handful of Dust,* Everyman's Library, no. 252 (New York: Knopf, 2002), 72.

5p   An Imprint

An imprint is a specialized division of a larger publishing company. When a publisher's name and an imprint name both appear on the title page, list them together (imprint second), separated by a comma.

>   1. Adetayo Adetago, *Telling Our Stories: Continuities and Divergencies in Black Autobiography* (New York: Macmillan, Palgrave, 2005), 107.

Macmillan is the publisher; Palgrave is the imprint.

5q   A Translation

A translator's name must always be included in a citation because he or she prepared the version of the work that you read. To emphasize the original work (the most common pattern), place the abbreviation *trans.* (for "translated by," not italicized) and the translator's name after the title (but following editors' names, if appropriate).

>   1. Mulder Arjeu, *Understanding Media Theory: Language, Image, Sound, Behavior,* trans. Laura Martz (New York: Distributed Art, 2004), 117.

If selections within a collection have different translators, the translator's name follows the selection. Placing the translator's name after the book title signals that he or she translated *all* selections in the collection.

>   2. Danilo Kiš, "Dogs and Books," trans. Duška Mikic-Mitchell, in *The Oxford Book of Jewish Stories,* ed. Ilan Stavans (New York: Oxford University Press, 1998), 325.

If you discuss techniques of translation, place the translator's name first, followed by a comma, the abbreviation *trans.* (not italicized), and the title of the work. If appropriate, follow the title with the author's or editor's name, introduced with *by* (not italicized).

3. Marcelle Thiébaux, trans., *The Writings of Medieval Women: An Anthology,* 2nd ed. (New York: Garland, 1994), xi–xii.

5r A Government Document— *Congressional Record*

Notes for *Congressional Record* include the title of the selection or section, the title *Congressional Record* spelled out in full (not abbreviated) and italicized, the volume number, the date in parentheses, a colon, and the page number. Page numbers used alone indicate Senate records; page numbers preceded by an *H* indicate records from the House of Representatives.

1. Introduction of the Campaign Spending Limit and Election Reform Act of 1993, *Congressional Record* 139 (June 15, 1993): 7276.
2. "Public School Statistics of the United States in 1880," table, *Congressional Record* 13 (June 13, 1882): H4825.

5s A Government Document—Committee, Commission, Department

Information describing government documents is generally presented in this order in citations: (1) country, state, province, or county (when necessary to avoid confusion); (2) governing body, sponsoring department, commission, center, ministry, or agency; (3) office, bureau, or committee; (4) the title of the publication, italicized; (5) if appropriate, the author of the document, the number and session of Congress, the kind and number of the document; (6) the city of publication, the publisher, and the date; and (7) the appropriate page or pages.

1. U.S. Congress, Budget Office, *Budget of the United States Government, Fiscal Year 2002* (Washington, DC: GPO, 2003), 13.

The Government Printing Office, the publisher of most federal documents, is abbreviated to save space.

    1. Commission on the Assassination of President Kennedy, *Investigation of the Assassination of President John F. Kennedy: Hearings before the President's Commission on the Assassination of President Kennedy,* vol. 3 (Washington, DC: GPO, 1964), 177–78.

Multivolume government documents (like this sixteen-volume collection) follow note patterns like those of other multivolume collections.

    2. Federal Reserve Board of Governors, *Bank Mergers and Banking Structure in the United States, 1980–98,* by Stephen A. Rhoades (Washington, DC: GPO, 2000), 55–56.

5t A Preface, Introduction, Foreword, Epilogue, or Afterword

To document material separate from the primary text, begin with the author's name, followed by a descriptive phrase like *introduction to* (not italicized), the title of the book, the name of the author of the book (introduced with *by,* also not italicized), publication facts, and appropriate page numbers. Note that the page numbers for most prefatory or introductory material are lowercase roman numerals.

    1. Harry J. Elam Jr., "(W)righting History: A Meditation in Four Beats," introduction to *The Past and Present in the Drama of August Wilson* (Ann Arbor: University of Michigan Press, 2004), 4–5.

This introduction has a formal title, which is included within quotation marks, followed by the descriptive title. Notice that Elam's book uses arabic numerals for the introduction's paging, rather than the more typical roman numerals.

    2. Richard Ellis, conclusion to *To the Flag: The Unlikely History of the Pledge of Allegiance* (Lawrence: University Press of Kansas, 2005), 220.
    3. William E. Leuchtenburg, foreword to *That Man: An Insider's Portrait of Franklin D. Roosevelt,* by Robert H. Jackson, ed. John Q. Barrett (New York: Oxford University Press, 2003), ix.

5u   A Pamphlet or Brochure

When pamphlets contain clear and complete information, they are presented the way books are. When information is missing, use these abbreviations: *n.p.* for "no place of publication," "no publisher," or "no page"; use *n.d.* for "no date." These abbreviations are not italicized in notes.

> 1. Mike Wyatt, *Taking Off: A Guide to Backpacking Trails across North America* (Emmaus, PA: Rodale, 1990), 3.
> 2. *Lyme Disease and Related Disorders* (Groton, NY: Pfizer, 2000), 3.

5v   Published Proceedings from a Conference

Begin a note for conference proceedings with the author's name, the title of the speech or paper (in quotation marks), a descriptive title if the speech had a special conference role (for example, *keynote address,* not italicized), the title of the conference if not already clear, the sponsoring group (if helpful), and the facts of publication.

> 1. John A. Rich, "The Health Crisis of Young Black Men in the Inner City," in *The Crisis of the Young African American Male in the Inner City,* United States Commission on Civil Rights, April 15–16, 1999 (Washington, DC: GPO, 2000), 136–37.
> 2. *Proceedings: The First National Conference on Visual Literacy,* ed. Clarence M. Williams and John L. Debes III (New York: Pitman, 1970).

The second note refers to the entire collected proceedings.

5w   A Dissertation

Begin a note for an unpublished dissertation with the author's name and the title, in quotation marks. In parentheses, include the description *Ph.D. diss.* (not italicized), a comma, the degree-granting university, and the date. The note ends with the page reference, outside the closing parenthesis.

> 1. Harriet L. Parnet, "The Terror of Our Days: Four American Poets Respond to the Holocaust" (Ph.D. diss., Lehigh University, 2000), 111.

A published dissertation is presented like a book (see section **5a**).

5x A Book Written in a Language Other than English

A note for a book written in a foreign language varies from normal patterns in several ways. When listing the title, use sentence-style capitalization. Second, include all accents and diacritical marks; if your printer does not offer such options, add them neatly by hand in black ink.

Include an English translation of the title in brackets following the foreign-language title. The English version of the title is capitalized headline style; it is neither italicized nor placed in quotation marks.

> 1. Jean Genet, *Les bonnes* [The Maids], in *Oeuvres complètes* [Complete Works] (Paris: Gallimard, 1968), 175–76.
> 2. Manuel Puig, *El beso de la mujer araña* [The Kiss of the Spider Woman] (Barcelona: Seix Barral, 1976), 22.

5y Sacred Writings

Notes for sacred writings follow patterns similar to those for other books, with several notable variations. First, titles of sacred writings (the parts or the whole) are neither placed in quotation marks nor italicized; they are simply capitalized in headline style. Second, full facts of publication are not required for traditional editions. When appropriate, include additional information according to the guidelines for the element.

> 1. The Bhagavad Gita, trans. Juan Mascaró (New York: Penguin Books, 1962), 2:13.
> 2. Psalm 23:3–6.

The second note is for the King James version of the Bible, the traditional English-language edition; other editions are indicated in parentheses after the line numbers but before the closing period, as in the sample below.

> 3. Psalm 23:3–6 (New English Bible).

5z   A Secondary Source

The authors of primary sources report their own research and ideas; the authors of secondary sources report the research and ideas of others. For example, William O. Stoddard, Abraham Lincoln's secretary, wrote journal entries regarding Lincoln's actions; his collected writing is a primary source. In 2005, Doris Kearns Goodwin used quotations from Stoddard's collected writing in a book on Lincoln's administration; her book is a secondary source. Although it is best to use the original or primary source (Stoddard), at times you must use the secondary source (Goodwin).

If you cannot locate the primary (original) source and must use the information from a secondary source, the reference note must include information for both the primary and secondary sources. In the text of the paper, refer to the primary source. Begin the reference note with the primary source; then introduce information for the secondary source with phrases such as *quoted in* or *cited in* (not italicized).

1. William O. Stoddard, *Dispatches from Lincoln's White House: The Anonymous Civil War Journalism of Presidential Secretary William O. Stoddard,* ed. Michael Burlingame (Lincoln: University of Nebraska Press, 2002), quoted in Doris Kearns Goodwin, *Team of Rivals: The Political Genius of Abraham Lincoln* (New York: Simon, 2005), 524–25.

Preparing Note Forms for Periodicals

Note Forms for Periodicals

6a An Article in a Journal with Continuous Paging
6b An Article in a Journal with Separate Paging
6c An Article in a Monthly Magazine
6d An Article in a Weekly Magazine
6e An Article in a Newspaper
6f An Editorial or a Letter to the Editor
6g A Review
6h An Abstract from *Dissertation Abstracts International*
6i A Secondary Source

Most often affiliated with professional organizations, journals are scholarly publications whose articles are subjected to careful review. Often called refereed journals, they are the mainstay of much research because they present ideas and information developed by scholars and specialists—and reviewed by scholars—for an audience of scholars. Magazines, by contrast, are commercial publications that present ideas and information for general readers who are nonspecialists; they provide nontechnical discussions and general reactions to issues. Newspapers—published daily or weekly—provide nearly instantaneous reactions to issues in primary stories and more reflective discussions in editorials and featured articles. These periodicals provide recent discussions of ideas and issues, as well as reports of research of importance to writers of researched papers.

To prepare reference notes for periodicals, follow the guidelines given in this chapter.

6a An Article in a Journal with Continuous Paging

A journal with continuous paging numbers an entire year's worth of journals consecutively, even though there are separately numbered issues. For example, *Social History's* volume 30 (representing 2005) has numbered issues that are continuously paged: issue number 1 (February 2005) includes pages 1–132, number 2 (May 2005) spans pages 133–280, number 3 (August 2005) continues with pages 281–419, and so on.

When an article comes from a journal with continuous paging, list author, article title (in quotation marks), and journal title (in italics), separated by commas. Place the volume number (not italicized) one space after the journal title, identify the year (or month or season and year) in parentheses, follow it with a colon, and then list page numbers.

1. Sally Bick, "*Of Mice and Men:* Copland, Hollywood, and American Musical Modernism," *American Music* 23 (2005): 426.

2. Aurora Sherman, Brian de Vries, and Jennifer E. Lansford, "Friendship in Childhood and Adulthood: Lessons across the Life Span," *International Journal of Aging and Human Development* 51 (2000): 50.

6b An Article in a Journal with Separate Paging

A journal with separate paging begins each numbered issue with page 1, even though a year's worth of journals is assigned a single volume number. For example, *African Studies Review's* volume 48 (representing 2005) has numbered issues, each of which has separate paging: issue number 1 includes pages 1–236, issue number 2 spans pages 1–201, issue number 3 covers pages 1–232, and so on.

When journals page each issue separately, follow the volume number with a comma and the issue number, identified with the abbreviation *no.* (not italicized); all else remains the same.

1. Wayne Barrett, "G. F. Handel's *Messiah:* Drama Theolicus: A Discussion of *Messiah's* Text with Implications for Its Performance," *Choral Journal* 46, no. 6 (2005): 13.

2. Michael G. Sargent, "Mystical Writings and Dramatic Texts in Late Medieval England," *Religion and Literature* 37, no. 2 (2005): 83.

6c An Article in a Monthly Magazine

The note for a monthly magazine requires the author's name, the article's title in quotation marks, the name of the magazine (italicized), the month (either spelled out or abbreviated, as long as the pattern is used consistently in both notes and bibliographic citations) and year, and appropriate pages.

1. Janet Koplos, "Portraits of Light," *Art in America,* February 2006, 87.

2. Gregory Chaitin, "The Limits of Reason," *Scientific American,* March 2006, 75.

6d An Article in a Weekly Magazine

Notes for articles in weekly magazines are identical to those for monthly magazines, with one exception: the publication date is presented in more detailed form.

1. Janet Malcolm, "The Art of Testifying: The Confirmation Hearings as Theatre," *New Yorker,* March 13, 2006, 71.

2. Nikki Stern, "Our Grief Doesn't Make Us Experts," *Newsweek,* March 13, 2006, 20.

6e An Article in a Newspaper

Notes for newspapers resemble those for magazines: they include the author's name (if known), article title (in quotation marks), newspaper title (italicized), and the date. Pages may be omitted.

When newspapers are divided into sections, provide clarifying information either after the newspaper title or after the date.

1. Francis Davis, "Strata Various," *Village Voice,* March 8–14, 2006.

2. Peter Sanders, "How to Buy a College Team," *Wall Street Journal,* March 13, 2006.

3. Gare Joyce, "Moving Heaven and (Middle) Earth," *Christian Science Monitor,* March 10, 2006.

6f An Editorial or a Letter to the Editor

The note for an editorial is presented like one for a magazine or newspaper article, as is a note for a letter to the editor; for clarity, the word *editorial* or phrase *letter to the editor* (neither one italicized), follows the title, with commas before and after.

    1. George F. Will, "Professors of Pretense," editorial, *Washington Post*, March 8, 2006.

    2. Elliott Eisenberg, letter to the editor, *Chicago Tribune*, sec. 1, March 8, 2006.

6g A Review

Reviews begin with the author's name and the title of the review, if any. The phrase *review of* (not italicized) follows, with the name of the book, film, album, performance, product, or whatever else is being reviewed. Publication information ends the note, incorporating elements required for different kinds of sources.

    1. Gustavo Guerra, review of *Pragmatism, Postmodernism, and the Future of Philosophy,* by John J. Stuhr, *Journal of Speculative Philosophy* 19 (2005): 274–76.

    2. Eileen M. Otis, "The Gender of Global Politics," review of *The Curious Feminist: Searching for Women in a New Age of Empire,* by Cynthia Enloe, *Contexts* 4, no. 3 (2005): 68–70.

6h An Abstract from *Dissertation Abstracts International*

Include the author's name; the title of the dissertation (in quotation marks); the degree and degree-granting university, in parentheses; the title *Dissertation Abstracts International* and the volume number; the year, in parentheses; and the identification number.

    1. Margarita Dikovitskaya, "From Art to Visual Culture: The Study of the Visual after the Cultural Turn" (Ph.D. diss., Columbia University), *Dissertation Abstracts International* 62 (2002), AAT3028516.

6i A Secondary Source

The authors of primary sources report their own research and ideas; the authors of secondary sources report the research and ideas of others. For example, Kathleen M. McGraw conducted her own study of voters' reactions to political candidates and reported her findings in an essay in 2003; it is a primary source. In 2005, James N. Druckman and Michael Parkin incorporated material from McGraw's essay in an article for *The Journal of Politics;* it is a secondary source. Although it is best to use the original or primary source (McGraw), at times you must use the secondary source (Druckman and Parkin).

If you cannot locate the primary (original) source and must use the information from a secondary source, the reference note must include information for both the primary and secondary sources. In the text of the paper, refer to the primary source. Begin the reference note with the primary source; then introduce information for the secondary source with phrases such as *quoted in* or *cited in* (not italicized).

1. Kathleen M. McGraw, "Political Impressions," in *Political Psychology,* ed. David O. Sears, Leonie Huddy, and Robert Jervis, 394–432 (Oxford: Oxford University Press, 2003), quoted in James N. Druckman and Michael Parkin, "The Impact of Media Bias: How Editorial Slant Effects Voters," *Journal of Politics* 67 (2005): 1032.

7 Preparing Note Forms for Audiovisual Sources

Note Forms for Audiovisual Sources

7a A Film
7b A Filmstrip
7c A Television Broadcast
7d A Radio Broadcast
7e A Recording
7f A Performance
7g An Interview
7h A Transcript
7i A Lecture or Speech
7j A Work of Art
7k An Exhibit
7l A Map, Graph, Table, or Chart
7m A Cartoon

Finding the documentation information for audiovisual sources is usually easy but sometimes requires ingenuity. CD cases provide the manufacturers' catalog numbers and copyright dates. Both printed programs for speeches and syllabuses for course lectures provide names, titles, locations, and dates. Information about films or television programs can be obtained from their opening or closing credits, from reference books, or from a variety of online sources. If you have difficulty in finding the information to document audiovisual sources clearly, ask your instructor or a librarian for help.

7a A Film

When referring to a film as a complete work, include the director's name (with the abbreviation *dir.* —not italicized), the title (italicized), publishing information (the city, company, and date, all in parentheses), and a format label. If you include other people's contributions, do so after the title, using brief phrases (*produced by, with, original score by, edited by*—not italicized) to clarify their roles; indicate a nonfilm format (DVD, videocassette) after the title but before contributors.

1. Ang Lee, dir., *Brokeback Mountain,* with Heath Ledger, Jake Gyllenhaal, and Michelle Williams (Los Angeles, CA: Focus Features, River Road Entertainment, 2005), film.

2. David Fincher, dir., *Fight Club,* DVD, with Brad Pitt, Edward Norton, and Helena Bonham Carter (Hollywood, CA: 20th Century Fox, Regency, 1999).

When a film has a dual release, include the names of both studios separated by commas.

7b   A Filmstrip

Filmstrips are identified as films are.

1. *The Great American Deficit: Mortgaging the Future,* Current Affairs Series (New York: Contemporary Media, New York Times, 1986), filmstrip.

This filmstrip is part of a series; it is also co-produced.

2. *Selected Masterpieces of Asian Art: 1890–1990* (Boston: Museum of Fine Art, 2001), filmstrip. 250 slides.

7c   A Television Broadcast

Regular programs are listed by title (italicized), the network (CBS, CNN, FOX), and the broadcast date. List other contributors after the program title, using brief phrases (*narrated by, with, written by*—not italicized) to clarify their roles.

1. *Empire Falls,* with Ed Harris, Helen Hunt, Joanne Woodward, Paul Newman, Robin Wright Penn, Aidan Quinn, and Philip Seymour Hoffman, HBO, May 5, 2005.

To cite an episode of a program, include the episode's name in quotation marks before the program's title. Other elements are presented in the same order as is used for a regular program.

2. "Take Your Daughter to Work Day," *The Office,* with Steve Carell, Jenna Fischer, John Krasinski, B. J. Novak, and Rainn Wilson, NBC, March 16, 2006.

7d   A Radio Broadcast

A note for a radio broadcast follows the guidelines for a television broadcast.

> 1. "The War of the Worlds," with Orson Welles, WCBS, October 30, 1938.

7e   A Recording

Notes for recordings usually begin with the performer or composer, followed by the title of the album (italicized except for titles using numbers for musical form, key, or number), the recording format, the record company, and the catalog number. Although it is not required, a publication or copyright date can be added after the catalog number, using the symbols ℗ or ©. List other contributors after the title, using brief phrases (*conducted by, with, composed by*—not italicized) to clarify their roles; orchestras and other large musical groups are listed without clarifying phrases and usually follow the conductor's name or the title of the album.

Indicate the recording format (compact disc, audiotape, record) before the company name. The information about multidisc sets, similar to the pattern for multivolume books, appears immediately preceding the catalog number.

> 1. The Beatles, *Abbey Road*, compact disc, Capital-EMI CDp7-46446-2, ℗ 1969.
> 2. William Bolcom, *Songs of Innocence and Experience*, conducted by Leonard Slatkin, University of Michigan School of Music Symphony Orchestra, compact disc, Naxos 8559216-18, ℗ 2004.
> 3. Gustav Mahler, Symphony no. 1 in D major, conducted by Georg Solti, Chicago Symphony Orchestra, record, London 411731-2, ℗ 1984.

A note for a single selection from a recording includes the selection title in quotation marks just before the title of the complete recording, introduced by the word *on* (not italicized). All else remains the same.

> 4. Dwight Yoakam, "An Exception to the Rule," on *Population ME*, compact disc, Audium 8-81762-7, ℗ 2003.

Extensive use of music or musical texts as the basis for research work necessitates the presentation of a discography, a citation list of exclusively musical sources (see *Chicago Manual of Style*'s section 17.267).

7f A Performance

A note for a performance usually begins with the title of the work being performed, provides information about contributors, and ends with the facility (theater, center, auditorium, performance hall, or other venue), city (and state, if needed for clarity), and performance date. To create other emphasis, the note can begin with the name of a contributor.

1. *Long Day's Journey into Night,* written by Eugene O'Neill, with Vanessa Redgrave, Brian Dennehy, Robert Sean Leonard, and Philip Seymour Hoffman, Plymouth Theatre, New York, August 17, 2003.

2. Boston Symphony Orchestra, Fourth Symphony, by Johannes Brahms, conducted by Emmanuel Krivine, with Joshua Bell, Symphony Hall, Boston, April 1, 2006.

7g An Interview

Notes for personally conducted interviews include the name of the person interviewed, the phrase *interview by author* (not italicized), and the interview place and date, when applicable. Clarifying information may be added when appropriate.

1. Stephen Otwell, interview by author, Cook County Library, Chicago, February 14, 2006.

2. Richard Lindley, telephone interview by author, May 13, 2006.

Notes for broadcast or printed interviews begin with the name of the person who was interviewed and the interviewer, followed by the program title, if applicable. The remaining portion of the note should follow the pattern required for the source.

3. William F. Buckley Jr., interview by Charlie Rose, *The Charlie Rose Show,* PBS, March 24, 2006.

7h   A Transcript

Transcripts of programs are presented according to the
source of the original broadcast, with the word *transcript*
(not italicized) after the program name.

> 1. Kathleen Koch, *Saving My Town: The Fight for Bay
St. Louis,* transcript, *CNN Presents,* CNN, February 26, 2006.

7i   A Lecture or Speech

A note for a lecture includes the speaker's name and the
title of the lecture (in quotation marks) or a descriptive
phrase presented in headline-style capitalization. In
parentheses, place the name of the lecture series or context for the speech (if applicable), the location of the
speech (university, library, meeting hall), the city (and
state, if necessary), and the date.

> 1. Paul Bebbington, "Who's the Greatest? Minds That
Changed Our Minds" (lecture, Royal Institution, London,
April 27, 2006).
> 2. Richard Nixon, Resignation Speech (speech, White
House, Washington, DC, August 8, 1974).

7j   A Work of Art

When artists' names are known and the artists have titled
their own work, include this information: artist's name;
the title (italicized); a description of the work; the date of
the work; the museum, gallery, or collection where the
work of art is housed; and the city (and state, province, or
country, if needed for clarity).

When a work of art is included as an illustration (figure) within the text, the information that would otherwise appear in a reference note is placed in parentheses
after the figure caption (see page 28).

> 1. Paul Gauguin, *The Brooding Woman,* oil on canvas,
1891, Worcester Art Museum, Worcester, MA.

When works of art are known primarily by titles in foreign languages, provide the original title in italics (with
sentence-style capitalization), followed by the translated

title in brackets (capitalized headline style without italics). All else remains the same.

2. Henri de Toulouse-Lautrec, *La clownesse assise* [The Seated Clown], oil on canvas, 1895, Marie Harriman Gallery, New York.

7k An Exhibit

Notes for exhibits include the title, the word *exhibit* set off by commas but neither italicized nor placed in quotation marks, the name of the museum or facility, the city (and state if needed for clarity), and the viewing date.

1. "Life in the Shadows: Hidden Children and the Holocaust," exhibit, Museum of Jewish Heritage, New York, May 1, 2006.
2. "Impressionist Camera: Pictorial Photography in Europe, 1888–1918," exhibit, St. Louis Art Museum, April 2006.

7l A Map, Graph, Table, or Chart

Maps, graphs, tables, and charts are treated like books. If known, include the name of the author, artist, designer, scientist, or other person—or group—responsible for the map, graph, table, or chart. Include the title as it appears in the source, italicized, followed by a descriptive title. Then include the information required for your source.

When a map, graph, table, or chart is included as an illustration (figure) within the text, the information that would otherwise appear in a reference note is placed in parentheses after the figure caption (see page 28).

1. *Weighty Matters,* graph, "The Politics of Fat," by Karen Tumulty, *Time,* March 27, 2006, 42.

This graph is part of an article in a magazine.

2. Kevin L. Phillips, *A Growing Income Disparity,* chart, *Wealth and Democracy: A Political History of the American Rich* (New York: Broadway, 2002), 129.

This chart is part of a book.

7m   A Cartoon

Begin with the cartoonist's name; the caption of a single-cell cartoon or the title of a single cartoon strip (both in quotation marks) or the title of a cartoon series (in italics), and the word *cartoon* (not italicized). Then include the publication information required for the source.

When a cartoon is included as an illustration (figure) within the text, the information that would otherwise appear in a reference note is placed in parentheses after the figure caption (see page 28).

    1. Bek, "I don't know if he's a great artist, but he's certainly annoying," cartoon, *New Yorker,* August 11, 2003, 60.

    2. Jack Davis and Stan Hart, "Groan with the Wind," cartoon, *Mad,* January 1991, 42.

8 Preparing Note Forms for Electronic Sources

Note Forms for Electronic Sources

8a An Online Scholarly Project, Information Database, or Professional Web Site

8b A Source from an Online Scholarly Project, Information Database, or Professional Web Site

8c An Online Book

8d An Article in an Online Journal

8e An Article in an Online Magazine

8f An Article in an Online Newspaper

8g An Article in an Online Encyclopedia or Other Reference Work

8h An Online Government Document

8i An Online Transcript of a Lecture or Speech

8j An Online Work of Art

8k An Online Exhibit

8l An Online Map, Graph, Table, or Chart

8m An Online Transcript of a Television or Radio Broadcast

8n An Online Audio Source

8o A CD-ROM Source

8p An E-mail Interview

8q An Online Posting

Electronic sources exist in many formats—scholarly projects, online databases, electronic publications of traditional print sources, organizational Web sites, CD-ROMs, e-mail-based discussion groups, and others. To allow researchers to cite these sources, Chicago has adopted the relatively straightforward strategy of, first, following note patterns that exist for comparable print sources and, second, adding information about electronic access.

As you gather citation information for electronic sources, you must be resourceful in finding important information; your goal should be to provide the most complete set of information possible for each electronic source, following the patterns described in this section.

If a source's URL extends beyond one line, break it after a slash (/) or a double slash (//); before a period, a hyphen, an underline, a question mark, or a tilde (~); or either before or after an equals sign or an ampersand (&).

Specialized Online Sources

Online sources exist in many forms. Although they are
all designed in approximately the same way—with a
home page that directs users to subsites where information can be found—some specialized sites have
distinct purposes and applications and, consequently,
need to be cited in distinct ways.

- *Online scholarly projects.*   Often affiliated with uni-
  versities, foundations, and governmental agencies,
  these sites are depositories of resources as varied as
  articles, books, digitized images of original documents, recordings, and even film clips. Because their
  affiliations help establish their credibility, that information is often included in reference notes and bibliographic entries.

- *Information databases.*   Typically developed by governmental agencies or by information-technology
  firms, these sites provide access to cataloged information that is accessed by using keyword
  search terms. Periodical databases like ProQuest,
  EBSCOhost, LexisNexis, JSTOR, and WorldCat make
  periodical articles available in a variety of formats
  (see section 1d); other databases provide access to
  cataloged music, art, historic documents, and so on.
  Because of their role as "providers" of this material,
  reference notes and bibliographic entries often include the agency or company name and the version,
  edition, revision, or posting date.

- *Professional Web sites.*   Affiliated with professional
  organizations in virtually every discipline, these sites
  make materials available that support or enhance
  the work of the organization—research documents,
  online resources, Web links, news items, press re-
  leases, and so on. Web site titles typically include the
  organization's name; if they do not, this information
  should be added for clarity.

8a An Online Scholarly Project, Information Database, or Professional Web Site

To create a note for an entire online scholarly project, information database, or Web site, present available information in this order: (1) the title of the project, database, or Web site, not italicized; (2) the editor or compiler, if identified, introduced with the abbreviation *ed.* or *comp.* and not italicized; (3) the city, "publisher" (sponsor, affiliated institution, or corporation), and publication or posting date—all in parentheses; (4) the electronic address (URL); and (5) an access note in parentheses.

1. The On-line Books Page, ed. John Mark Ockerbloom (Philadelphia: University of Pennsylvania, 2006), http://digital.library.upenn.edu/books (accessed March 15, 2006).
2. Thomas: Legislative Information on the Internet (Washington, DC: Library of Congress, 2006), http://thomas.loc.gov (accessed January 15, 2006).

8b A Source from an Online Scholarly Project, Information Database, or Professional Web Site

To create a note for a selected source—article, illustration, map, and so on—from an online scholarly project, information database, or Web site, begin with (1) the name of the author (or artist, compiler, or editor) of the individual source, if appropriate, and (2) the title of the source, punctuated accordingly (quotation marks for articles, italics for charts, and so on). Continue the note with the name of the online project, database, or Web site and other required information.

1. Franklin Roosevelt, "A Date Which Will Live in Infamy": Joint Address to Congress (speech, U. S. Congress, Washington, DC, December 8, 1941), America's Historical Documents, National Archives and Record Administration (College Park, MD: NARA, 2005), http://www.archives.gov/historical-docs/ (accessed April 3, 2006).
2. David Cody, "Queen Victoria," The Victorian Web, ed. George P. Landow (Providence, RI: Brown University, December 12, 2002), http://www.victorianweb.org.vn/victor6.html (accessed March 11, 2006).

8c An Online Book

Online books exist in two forms: those previously published and now available electronically and those available only in electronic form.

To prepare a note for an online book that has a corresponding print version, first complete a standard note
describing the print version (see chapter 5). Then provide
additional electronic information required for a scholarly
project, information database, or Web site, as appropriate
(see section **8a**).

    1. Hugh Lofting, *The Voyages of Doctor Dolittle*
(Philadelphia: Lippincott, 1922), Project Gutenberg (Urbana:
University of Illinois, 1998), http://www.Gutenberg.org/dirs/
etext98/vdrdl10.txt (accessed February 24, 2006).

    2. Hugh Witemeyer, *George Eliot and the Visual Arts*
(New Haven, CT: Yale University Press, 1979), The Victorian
Web, ed. George P. Landow (Providence, RI: Brown
University, 2000), http://www.victorianweb.org/authors/
eliot/nw/contents.html (accessed January 15, 2006).

A note for an online book that is available only in electronic form includes (1) the name of the author or editor;
(2) the title, italicized; and (3) the information required for
the scholarly project, information database, or Web site.

    1. Sophie Buxhoeveden, *The Life and Tragedy of
Alexandra Feodorvna, Empress of Russia,* Russian History
Web Site (1999), http://www.alexanderpalace.org/alexandra
(accessed January 11, 2006).

A note for a selection from an online book—a chapter
from a book, an essay or poem from a collection, and so
on—provides this information: (1) the author of the selection and (2) the title of the selection, in quotation marks or
italicized, as appropriate. The note then continues with
the information required for the scholarly project, information database, or Web site (see section **8a**).

    1. A. E. Housman, "To an Athlete Dying Young," in
A Shropshire Lad (London: Paul, 1896), Bartleby.com (2006),
http://www.bartleby.com/123/19.html (accessed April 2, 2006).

8d An Article in an Online Journal

To present a note for an article in an online journal, supply (1) the name of the author, if appropriate; (2) the title
of the article, in quotation marks; (3) the name of the

journal, italicized, and the volume and issue number, as needed; (4) the year of electronic publication or of the most recent update, in parentheses; (5) the URL; and (6) an access note in parentheses.

1. Robb Willer, "The Effects of Government-Issued Terror Warnings on Presidential Approval Ratings," *Current Research in Social Psychology* 10, no. 1 (2004), http://www.uiowa.edu/%7Egrpproc/crisp/prior.html (accessed April 6, 2006).

2. Nicholas Jabbour, "Syphilis from 1880 to 1920: A Public Health Nightmare and the First Challenge to Medical Ethics," *Essays in History* 42 (2000), http://www.etext.lib.virginia.edu/journals/eh/eh42/jabbour42.html (accessed March 16, 2006).

3. John Milton Cooper Jr., review of *When Trumpets Call: Theodore Roosevelt after the White House* by Patricia O'Toole, *Journal of American History* 92 (2006): 1466, ProQuest (2006), http://umi.com/pqdweb?index=6&did=1013751671&SrchMode=1&sid=3&Fmt=3 (accessed May 14, 2006).

8e An Article in an Online Magazine

A note for an article in an online magazine includes (1) the name of the author, if appropriate; (2) the title of the article, in quotation marks; (3) the name of the magazine, italicized; (4) the date of electronic publication or the date of the most recent update; (5) the URL; and (6) an access note in parentheses.

1. Doug Stewart, "Resurrecting Pompeii," *Smithsonian,* February 2006, http://www.smithsonianmagazine.com/issues/2006/February/Pompeii.php?page=1 (accessed March 22, 2006).

2. Antonia Francis, "Fighting for the Rainforests," *Newsweek,* March 24, 2006, http://www.msnbc.msn.com/1d/120000362/site/newsweek/ (accessed March 26, 2006).

3. Dahir Mubarak, "Censoring History," *Advocate,* January 3, 2004, EBSCOhost (2006), http://web19.epnet.com/citation.asp?tb=1&_ug=sid+ACDC8D54%2DD0D0%2D4C3F%2 (accessed May 1, 2006).

8f An Article in an Online Newspaper

A note for an article in an online newspaper includes (1) the name of the author, if appropriate; (2) the title of the article, in quotation marks; (3) the name of the newspaper, italicized; (4) the date of electronic publication or the date of the most recent update; (5) the URL; and (6) an access note in parentheses.

1. Phillip O'Connor and Eun Kyung Kim, "Illegal Workers: Gain or Drain?" *St. Louis Post Dispatch,* April 1, 2006, http://www.stltoday.com/stltoday/news/stories/nsf/stlouiscitycounty/story/30333179F95C576B2862571430075A5FF?OpenDocument (accessed April 3, 2006).

2. Lianne Hart, "Getting Out the Displaced Vote," *Los Angeles Times,* April 2, 2006, http://www.latimes.com/news/nationworld/nation/la-na-absentee2apr02,1,1797413.story?coll=la-headlines-national&ctrack=18&cset=true (accessed April 2, 2006).

3. "Talking Spanish and Walking Saxon," *New York Daily Times,* May 7, 1852, 2, ProQuest Historical Newspapers (2006), http://proquest.umi.com/pqdweb?index=0&did=74959022&srchMode=1&sid=1&Fmt=10 (accessed May 22, 2006).

8g An Article in an Online Encyclopedia or Other Reference Source

A note for an article from an online encyclopedia or reference source supplies (1) the title of the electronic source, italicized; (2) the abbreviation *s.v.* for *sub verso* (meaning "under the word," not italicized); (3) the term as it appears in the reference work, in quotation marks; (4) the URL; and (5) an access note in parentheses.

1. *Infoplease Almanac,* s.v. "Children in Foster Care," http://www.infoplease.com/ipa/A0778809.html (accessed March 22, 2006).

2. *The New Dictionary of Cultural Literacy,* 3rd ed., s.v. "Carnegie, Andrew," Bartleby.com (2002), http://www.bartleby.com/59/18/carnegieandr.html (accessed May 10, 2006).

8h An Online Government Document

A note for an online version of a government document—book, report, proceedings, brochure, and so on—first provides the information required for the print source (see sections **5r** and **5s**). It then continues with the information appropriate to the electronic source, whether it is an information database or Web site (see section **8a**).

1. U.S. Congress, Budget Office, *Immigration Policy in the United States,* Congressional Budget Office (Washington, DC: GPO, February 2006), http://www.cbo.gov/ftpdocs/70xx/doc7051/02-28-Immigration.pdf (accessed March 6, 2006).

2. U. S. National Archives and Record Administration, "Pictures of World War II," National Archives and Record Administration (College Park, MD: National Archives and Record Administration, 2004), http://www.archives.gov/research/ww2/photos/#top (accessed April 9, 2006).

8i   An Online Transcript of a Lecture or Speech

To prepare a note for a transcript of a speech or lecture, first provide the information required for a lecture or speech (see section **7i**). Then include (1) the URL and (2) an access note in parentheses.

1. William Faulkner, Nobel Prize in Literature Acceptance (speech, Nobel Prize Ceremony, Stockholm, December 10, 1950), http://www.historyplace.com/speeches/faulkner.htm (accessed February 1, 2006).

2. Václav Havel, "The Emperor Has No Clothes" (speech, Library of Congress, Washington, DC, May 24, 2005), http://www.vaclavhavel.cz/index.php?sec=7&id=48kat=2&from=0 (accessed May 6, 2006).

8j   An Online Work of Art

To prepare a note for a work of art online, first provide information required for a work of art (see section **7j**). Then include (1) the URL and (2) an access note in parentheses.

1. Grant Wood, *American Gothic,* oil on beaverboard, 1930, Art Institute of Chicago, http://www.artic.edu/aic/collections/american/highlight_item?acc=1930.934&page=16 (accessed January 20, 2006).

2. Pablo Picasso, *Les Demoiselles d'Avignon,* oil on canvas, 1907, Museum of Modern Art, New York, http://www.moma.org/collection/browse_results.php?criteria=0%3AAD%3A%3A46098page_number=7&template_id=1&sort_order=1 (accessed March 28, 2006).

8k   An Online Exhibit

A note for an online exhibit begins with the information required for a traditional exhibit (see section **7k**). Next, include (1) the URL and (2) an access note in parentheses.

    1. "Cover Art: The *Time* Collection at the National Portrait Gallery," exhibit, National Portrait Gallery, Washington, DC, December 2005, http://www.npg.si.edu/time/ (accessed April 2, 2006).
    2. "Virtual Museum Tour," John F. Kennedy Presidential Library and Museum, Boston, 2005, http://jfklibrary.org/ (accessed March 23, 2006).

8l   An Online Map, Graph, Table, or Chart

To prepare a note for a map, graph, table, or chart online, first provide the information required for the kind of visual element (see section **7l**). Then continue the note with the information appropriate to the electronic source, whether it is a scholarly project, information database, or Web site (see section **8a**).

    1. *Families in Poverty by Size of Family and Number of Related Children: 2004,* table, Current Population Survey, 2005 Annual Social and Economic Supplement (Washington, DC: U. S. Census Bureau, 2005), http://pubdb3.census.gov/macro/032005/new37_000.htm (accessed April 8, 2006).
    2. "Michael Calcagno, *New York City Subway Map: May 29, 2005 Edition,* map, New York City Subway Route Maps (New York: New York City Subway, 2005), http://www.nycsubway.org/maps/route/ (accessed March 1, 2006).

8m   An Online Transcript of a Television or Radio Broadcast

A note for an online transcript of a television or radio broadcast includes (1) the title of the episode, if appropriate, in quotation marks; (2) the title of the program, italicized; (3) the broadcast company and the date of the original broadcast; (4) the URL; and (5) an access note in parentheses.

    1. "Supreme Ethics Problem," *Nightline,* with Cynthia McFadden, ABC, January 23, 2006, http://abcnews.go.com/Nightline/story?id=1541642 (accessed March 12, 2006).

2. "Wagner's 'Ring' Reimagined in America," *All Things Considered,* with Robert Siegel, NPR, March 24, 2006, http://www.npr.org/templates/story/story.php?storyId= 5298509 (accessed March 29, 2006).

8n   An Online Audio Source

Prepare a note for an online audio source according to the guidelines for the online source, whether it is a scholarly project, information database, or a professional Web site. After the title of the recording, provide a description: *audio recording, audio clip,* or some other similar phrase (not italicized).

1. "Martin Luther King Delivers 'I Have a Dream' Speech," audio recording, This Day in History (August 28, 1963), http://www.historychannel.com/broadband/ clipview/index.jsp?id=tdih_0828.54seconds (accessed March 29, 2006).

8o   A CD-ROM Source

If a CD-ROM source reproduces material available in print form, begin the citation with full print information: author (or editor), title, and facts of publication. If the material is not available in print form, provide (1) the author, if given; (2) the title, italicized; (3) the word *CD-ROM,* not italicized; and (4) the city, electronic publisher, and release date—all in parentheses.

1. Carol Sullivan Spafford, Augustus J. Itzo Pesce, and George S. Grosser, *Education Dictionary,* CD-ROM (Florence, KY: Delmar Learning, 2006).
2. Amanda Holden, Nicholas Kenyon, and Stephen Walsh, eds., *The Viking Opera Guide,* CD-ROM (London: Penguin Books, 1993).

8p   An E-mail Interview

A note for an e-mail interview follows the pattern of a traditional interview, with the word *e-mail* added (not italicized) for clarity.

1. Marla Washburne-Freise, e-mail interview by author, May 14, 2006.

8q   An Online Posting

To prepare a note for an online posting to a forum, discussion group, or blog, supply (1) the name of the author,
if known; (2) the official title of the posting, in quotation
marks; (3) the name of the forum, discussion group, or
blog; (4) the date of electronic publication or the date of
the most recent update; (5) the URL; and (6) an access
note in parentheses.

    1. "Threatened and Endangered Species Recovery
Act," Native Plants Forum, October 3, 2005, http://forums
.gardenweb.com/forums/load/natives/msg1013431130746
.html?26 (accessed January 14, 2006).

    2. Alexandre Enkerli, "Hegemonic Google and the
State of the Internet," Humanist Discussion Group, May 23,
2005, http://lists.village.Virginia.edu/lists_archive/
Humanist/v19/0046.html (accessed March 18, 2006).

At least 1-inch margin

INDIANA STATE UNIVERSITY

Matched spacing below first line and above last line

WALKING INTO HISTORY:
THE LEGACY OF THE LINCOLN MEMORIAL

Centered from top to bottom

HISTORY 332

BY
JARAH ESTES-COOPER

The title page is followed by a blank page.

APRIL 25, 2006

---

2 inches

All capitals, centered → WALKING INTO HISTORY:
THE LEGACY OF THE LINCOLN MEMORIAL

3 spaces →

I had seen it before, but only in pictures. It was in our history book. It was on a poster in Mr. McFarlan's government classroom. It was in a video I had watched in American history. It was in the books I had skimmed before the trip. But nothing prepared me for the feeling I got as I approached it with my fellow band members. We walked west along the reflecting pool, and it got larger and larger until we were standing at the foot of the steps, the steps that led to the Lincoln Memorial.

Anecdote as introductory strategy

Lead-in to thesis statement

As I looked up the steps at the front of the Memorial, I realized that I was, in a sense, walking

Centered page number (lead page) → 1

111

into the pictures, the posters, and the videos. Like thousands of people before me, I was walking into history. After all, the Lincoln Memorial is more than an impressive stone monument. Instead, it has become a symbol of American commemoration and demonstration.

Thesis statement

Plans to construct a memorial to Abraham Lincoln began in March 1867, when the United States Congress established the Lincoln Monument Association; however, the current site for the memorial was not chosen until 1901.[1] Designed by Henry Bacon to resemble a Greek temple, the rectangular Memorial's flat roof is supported by thirty-six columns, one for each state in the Union at the time of Lincoln's death, and texts of Lincoln's Gettysburg Address and second inaugural address are included on the south and north interior walls.[2] The nineteen-foot statue of Lincoln within the Memorial was designed by Daniel Chester French, who later observed, "The memorial tells you what manner of man you are coming to pay homage to: his simplicity, his grandeur, and his power."[3] Jules Guerin, who had done other commissioned work for the government, planned two murals: above the Gettysburg address, a mural was to "[depict] the angel of truth freeing a slave," while above the inaugural speech another mural would represent the unity of the North and South.[4]

Background information

Note number raised 1/2 space

Brackets to substitute depict for depicts

With designs complete, construction began on February 12, 1914, forty-nine years after Lincoln's assassination. The exterior was constructed of Colorado Yule marble and Tripods Pink Tennessee marble, while the interior used Indiana limestone and marble from

3

Alabama, Georgia, and Tennessee.[5] Progress was slow, and the Memorial was not completed until early 1922, at a cost of nearly three million dollars.[6] On May 20, 1922, President Warren G. Harding presided over the Memorial's dedication, which included a speech by Robert Morton, President of Tuskegee Institute; in attendance was Robert Todd Lincoln, President Lincoln's son.[7]

Transition paragraph

In the years that followed, thousands of visitors to the Capital climbed the vast staircase and walked within the Memorial, looking at the mammoth statue of the seated president, reading the carved speeches, and examining the murals. The responses were consistently positive, and the Lincoln Memorial became one of the most popular sites in Washington.

Surely part of the Memorial's appeal is its beauty, but another facet of its appeal rests in the ideals that it

Author and title to introduce quotation

represents. Leland M. Roth, in *Understanding Architecture: Its Elements, History, and Meaning,* asserts that the symbolic function of architecture "is most easily perceived in religious and public buildings where the principal intent is to make a broad and emphatic proclamation of communal values and beliefs."[8] In many ways, the Lincoln Memorial does proclaim "val-

Numerals used for measurements

ues and beliefs." Its size—99 feet high, 188 feet wide, and 118 feet deep—and simple design suggest grandeur and importance.[9] Its imposing statue of Lincoln shows a man who was, like the country, strong yet understanding: "One of the president's hands is clenched, representing his strength and determination to see the war to a successful conclusion. The other hand is an open, much more relaxed hand representing his compassionate[,] warm nature."[10] Charles L. Griswold, a

4

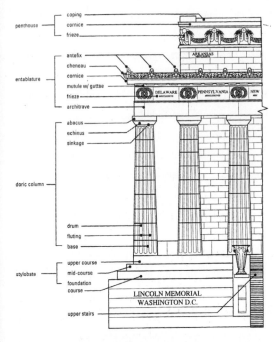

Fig. 1. Labeled architectural drawing. (From Elaine S. McGee's *Colorado Yule Marble: Building Stone of the Lincoln Memorial* [Washington, DC: GPO, 1999], vi.)

Figure with caption and source information

professor of philosophy at Boston University, comments on symbolic architecture in this way:

> [T]he architecture by which a people memorializes itself is a species of pedagogy. It therefore seeks to instruct posterity about the past and, in doing so, necessarily reaches a decision about what is worth recovering. . . . We must understand the monument's symbolism, social context, and the effects its architecture works on those who participate in it.[11]

Long quotation: set in 5 spaces, single-spaced

Writing specifically about the Lincoln Memorial, Griswold observes that "Lincoln's temple is, then, a

5

monument to national unity achieved by the martyrdom of Lincoln himself."[12]

Over the years, the Memorial has served a variety
of specific ceremonial functions. For example, at noon
on February 12 of each year, the current president
places a wreath at the side of Lincoln's statue. While
most presidents make only brief comments, some see
the ceremony as an opportunity to illustrate the symbolic principles of honoring Lincoln, as Harry Truman
did in 1947, when the traditional military color guard
was made nontraditional and highly symbolic: it was
composed of young black children.[13]

The commemorative nature of the Memorial
has been overshadowed on numerous occasions, however, by the use of the monument as a location for
demonstrations — both subtle and obvious. The
earliest of these demonstrations was on Easter Sunday,
1939. Marian Anderson, recognized throughout the
world as one of opera's greatest contraltos, was sched-
uled to perform in Washington, DC, but the Daughters
of the American Revolution (DAR), an all-white organization, denied her access to Constitution Hall.
Eleanor Roosevelt protested this action by resigning
her membership in the DAR, and within days the
Department of the Interior granted Anderson the right
to perform her concert on the steps of the Lincoln
Memorial.[14] Attended by 75,000 people, the concert
received extensive press coverage. Scott A. Sandage
notes in "A Marble House Divided: The Lincoln
Memorial, the Civil Rights Movement, and the Politics
of Memory: 1939–1963" that the concert was the first
large-scale gathering at the Memorial "to evoke lauda-
tory national publicity and earn a positive place in

Margin notes:

First example of activities

Facts and details incorporated into own language

Numerals used for subsequent comparisons

Sandage's words merged with writer's sentence

6

American public memory."[15] In subsequent years, other protests drew upon the impact of Anderson's performance, for it had "set the stage for future rallies and protests."[16]

Almost a decade later, the National Association for the Advancement of Colored People (NAACP) held the closing session of its thirty-eighth convention on the steps of the Lincoln Memorial.[17] Walter White, the NAACP president, and Eleanor Roosevelt sat in clear view as President Harry Truman delivered the closing address before 10,000 people.[18] Though the crowd was far smaller than that at the Anderson concert, the location of the address, with all of its symbolic associations, further helped to emphasize the role that the Memorial was to play in the civil rights movement.

Chronological transition

Perhaps the most-recognized event held at the Lincoln Memorial was the Civil Rights March on Washington in August 1963. The now-famous gathering was the closing event of a full day of activity. The demonstrators in the "March on Washington for Jobs and Freedom" began to gather at the Washington Monument in the morning while thirteen of their leaders spoke with congressional leaders; following these conversations, the leaders led the crowd westward through the National Mall toward the Lincoln Memorial.[19] Later in the day, ten of the leaders—representing religious, labor, and social- and political-action groups—spoke with President Kennedy while the crowd continued to grow.[20]

But what Americans know best is that Martin Luther King Jr.—the last of ten speakers—mesmerized the crowd, the nation, and the world while standing before the Lincoln Memorial.[21] King began his

7

King's speech
is common
knowledge

speech with a sentence that would stir memories and make clear his purpose: "Five score years ago, a great American, in whose symbolic shadow we stand today, signed the Emancipation Proclamation." The famous speech continued with other now-quotable lines, while the statue of "Lincoln brooded over his shoulder — the statue bathed in special lights to enhance its visibility on television and in news photographs."[22] The crowd was enormous — estimates range from 250,000 to 400,000 people — and the setting was ideal. For where else other than the Lincoln Memorial could King's point have been so powerfully made?

Another
time-related
transition

In less than a decade, the Lincoln Memorial became the backdrop for further protests, this time against American involvement in the Vietnamese War. On October 21, 1967, between 55,000 and 150,000 people (the numbers are highly disputed) attended a rally organized by the National Mobilization Committee to End the War in Vietnam.[23] The rally, which included a speech by Dr. Benjamin Spock (the famous pediatrician and author), was only the beginning of the protest; after the speeches, approximately 35,000 of the people marched to the Pentagon, where approximately 600 were arrested for disorderly behavior.[24]

Quotation
introduced by
name and
position

Two years later — on November 15, 1969 — another antiwar protest was held at the Lincoln Memorial. Plans were in place by late August; even the South Vietnamese ambassador Bui Diem knew of the upcoming demonstration and cabled South Vietnam's President Thieu this simple statement: "On November 15 they propose a great march, the 'March against Death.' "[25] Also known as the Vietnam

8

Fig. 2. Marchers at the Lincoln Memorial. (Photograph from United States, National Archives and Records Administration, "Civil Rights March on Washington, DC," National Archives and Records Administration [May 13, 1998], http://www.nara.gov/cgi-bin/ starfinder/17260/standards.txt [accessed April 3, 2006].)

Figure with caption and source information

War Moratorium, it drew approximately 600,000 people, making it the largest gathering of people in the history of the city.[26] The symbolism of hundreds of thousands of protestors singing "Give Peace a Chance" in front of the Lincoln Memorial was evident because by 1969, the Lincoln Memorial was clearly associated with American protests.[27]

    In the following decades, the Lincoln Memorial—and the area of the National Mall that spreads before it—has served as the location for many other protests and rallies: the AIDS quilt has been dis-

A brief account of other events

played each year since 1987, the Million Man March convened there in 1995, the Promise Keepers gathered there in 1997, and the Million Mom March protested against gun violence in 2000.[28] In addition, the Memorial has served as the location for a variety of recent public celebrations. It was the site of a 1999 New Year's concert that included a speech by President Clinton.[29] And in 2001, a two-and-a-half hour concert on the steps of the Memorial celebrated the inauguration of President Bush.[30]

In an article titled "Monuments in an Age without Heroes," Nathan Glazer reminds us that a "successful monument incorporates symbolic meanings . . . and can carry new meanings attributed to it over time without any necessary diminishment."[31] The Lincoln Memorial surely has done that. It remains a beautiful piece of architecture, one easily recognized in its hundreds of images in history and travel books, in film references, and even on the reverse side of the five-dollar bill. Yet because of its associations with commemorations, celebrations, and, most importantly, major demonstrations throughout the twentieth century, the Lincoln Memorial has assumed a symbolic role that few other national landmarks have achieved. Once, the Memorial was known as "The Temple of Democracy."[32] Through its varied use by the American people, it has become "The Temple of Our Democracy in Action."

Ellipsis points for omitted material

Revisiting images from the introduction

Modified quotation as concluding strategy

2 inches

All capitals centered   NOTES

3 spaces ———————————————→

Single-spaced;   1. United States, National Park Service, "Lincoln
double-   Memorial," Monuments and Memorials (1999),
spacing   http://www.nps.gov/linc/ (accessed March 29, 2006).
between

                        2. United States, National Park Service,
                   "Lincoln: The Memorial," Lincoln Memorial
                   (December 22, 2004), http://www.nps.gov/linc/
                   memorial/memorial.htm (accessed April 3, 2006).

                        3. United States, National Archives and Records
                   Administration, "The Unfinished Lincoln Memorial,"
                   National Archives and Records Administration (May
                   13, 1998), http://www.nara.gov/education/teaching/
                   memorial/memhome.html (accessed April 2, 2006).

Short forms   4. United States, National Park Service,
for later refer-   "Lincoln: The Memorial."
ences

                        5. United States, National Park Service, "Stones
                   and Mortar: The Statistics of the Monuments and
                   Memorial on the National Mall," National Park
                   Service (January 6, 2004), http://www.nps.gov/mall/
                   mortar/mortar.htm#linc (accessed April 3, 2006).

                        6. *Encarta Reference,* s.v. "Lincoln Memorial,"
                   http://encarta.msn.com/find/concise.asp?ti=
                   0697F000 (accessed March 26, 2006).

                        7. United States, National Park Service, "Lincoln
                   Memorial."

                        8. Leland M. Roth, *Understanding Architecture:
                   Its Elements, History, and Meaning* (New York: Icon-
                   Harper, 1993), 5.

                        9. United States, National Park Service, "Stones
                   and Mortar."

                        10. United States, National Park Service,
                   "Lincoln Memorial."

11

12

11. Charles L. Griswold, "The Vietnam Veterans
Memorial and the Washington Mall: Philosophical
Thoughts on Political Iconography," in *Critical Issues in
Public Art: Content, Context, and Controversy,* ed.
Harriet F. Senie and Sally Webster, 71–100 (Washington,
DC: Smithsonian Institution Press, 1992), 71–73.

12. Ibid., 80.   Same source,
                                                   different page

13. United States, National Archives and
Records Administration (May 13, 1998), http://www
.nara.gov/cgi-bin/starfinder/ (accessed April 5, 2006).

14. Jenny Allen, "Righteous Song in the Open
Air," *Life,* 1998, n.p., ProQuest (2006), http://proquest
.umi.com/pqdweb/ (accessed March 15, 2006).

15. Scott A. Sandage, "A Marble House Divided:
The Lincoln Memorial, the Civil Rights Movement,
and the Politics of Memory, 1939–1963," *Journal of
American History* 80 (1993): 157.

16. "Lincoln Memorial," The Mall (2005),
http://library.thinkquest.org/2813/mall/lincoln.html
(accessed March 20, 2006).

17. United States, National Archives and
Records Administration.

18. Ibid.   Same source,
                                                   same page

19. *Facts.com,* s.v. "Civil Rights: March on
Washington," http://www.2facts.com/stories/index/
h006707.asp (accessed April 2, 2006).

20. Ibid.

21. Ibid.

22. Sandage, 157.

23. *Facts.com,* s.v. "Vietnamese War Protests: First line in-
Washington Demonstrations," http://www.2facts.com/ dented; others
stories/index/h01825.asp (accessed April 1, 2006). at margin

24. Ibid.

25. Bui Diem, *In the Jaws of History,* with David Chanoff (Boston: Houghton, 1987), 268.

26. Cindy Hall, "Washington's Great Gatherings," *USA Today,* March 16, 2001, http://www .usatoday.com/news/index/mman006.htm (accessed March 20, 2006).

27. Jon Wiener, "Save the Mall," *Nation,* November 13, 2000, 8.

28. Ibid.

29. "2000 Washington, DC: Capital Thrills," *People,* January 17, 2000, ProQuest (2006), http:// proquest.umi.com/pqdweb/ (accessed March 16, 2006).

30. Jessie Halladay and Blake Morrison, "Martin Kicks Off Inaugural Festivities: Bush Shares Stage with Pop Sensation," *USA Today,* January 19, 2001, ProQuest (2006), http://proquest.umi.com/pqdweb/ (accessed April 1, 2006).

31. Nathan Glazer, "Monuments in an Age with- out Heroes," *Public Interest* 123 (1996), Proquest (2006), http://proquest.umi.com/pqdweb/ (accessed April 1, 2006).

32. United States, National Park Service, "Lincoln: The Memorial."

2 inches

BIBLIOGRAPHY

←————— 3 spaces

Allen, Jenny. "Righteous Song in the Open Air." *Life,*
1998, n.p. ProQuest (2006). http://proquest.umi
.com/pqdweb/ (accessed March 16, 2006).

Diem, Bui. *In the Jaws of History.* With David
Chanoff. Boston: Houghton, 1987.

Glazer, Nathan. "Monuments in an Age without
Heroes." *Public Interest* 123 (1996). Proquest
(2006). http://proquest.umi.com/pqdweb/ (accessed April 1, 2006).

Griswold, Charles L. "The Vietnam Veterans Memorial
and the Washington Mall: Philosophical Thoughts
on Political Iconography." In *Critical Issues in
Public Art: Content, Context, and Controversy,*
edited by Harriet F. Senie and Sally Webster,
71–100. Washington, DC: Smithsonian
Institution Press, 1999.

Hall, Cindy. "Washington's Great Gatherings." *USA
Today,* March, 16, 2001. http://www.usatoday
.com/news/index/mman006.htm (accessed March
20, 2006).

Halladay, Jessie, and Blake Morrison. "Martin Kicks
Off Inaugural Festivities: Bush Shares Stage with
Pop Sensation." *USA Today,* January 19, 2001.
ProQuest (2006). http://proquest.umi.com/
pqdweb/ (accessed April 1, 2006).

"Lincoln Memorial." The Mall (2005). http://library
.thinkquest.org/2813/mall/lincoln.html (accessed
March 20, 2006).

Alphabetized by first element

First line at margin; others indented

14

15

McGee, Elaine S. *Colorado Yule Marble: Building Stone of the Lincoln Memorial.* Washington, DC: GPO, 1999.

Roth, Leland M. *Understanding Architecture: Its Elements, History, and Meaning.* New York: Icon-Harper, 1993.

Sandage, Scott A. "A Marble House Divided: The Lincoln Memorial, the Civil Rights Movement, and the Politics of Memory, 1939–1963." *Journal of American History* 80 (1993): 135–67.

"2000 Washington, DC: Capital Thrills." *People,* January, 17, 2000. ProQuest (2006). http://proquest.umi.com/pqdweb/ (accessed March 16, 2006).

United States. National Archives and Records Administration (May 13, 1998). http://www.nara.gov/cgi-bin/starfinder/ (accessed April 5, 2006).

———. National Archives and Records Administration, "Civil Rights March on Washington, DC." Photograph. National Archives and Records Administration (May 13, 1998). http://www.nara.gov/cgi-bin/starfinder/17260/standards.txt (accessed April 3, 2006).

———. National Archives and Records Administration. "The Unfinished Lincoln Memorial." National Archives and Records Administration (May 13, 1998). http://www.nara.gov/education/teaching/memorial/memhome.html (accessed April 2, 2006)

———. National Park Service. "Lincoln Memorial." Monuments and Memorials (1999). http://www.nps.gov/linc/ (accessed March 29, 2006).

Numbers alphabetized as if spelled

Repeated elements with 3-em dash

16

———. National Park Service. "Lincoln: The Memorial." Lincoln Memorial (December 22, 2004). http://www.nps.gov/linc/memorial/memorial.htm (accessed April 3, 2006).

———. National Park Service. "Stones and Mortar: The Statistics of the Monuments and Memorial on the National Mall." National Park Service (January 6, 2004). http://www.nps.gov/mall/mortar/mortar.htm#linc (accessed April 3, 2006).

Weiner, Jon. "Save the Mall." *Nation,* November 13, 2000, 8.

A Parts of the Chicago-Style Paper

- *Title page.*   The opening page that highlights the title of the paper, provides identifying information about the author, and clarifies the context in which the paper was written.

- *Blank page.*   A blank page that prevents subsequent text pages from showing through to the title page.

- *Dedication.*   A brief statement on a separate page that names the person or people to whom the writer dedicates the work.

- *Epigraph.*   A quotation (listed only with the author's name) that has special value for the paper. Presented on a separate page, it may illustrate a crucial idea or in some way contextualize the paper.

- *Table of contents.*   A listing of major divisions of the work: chapters, long sections of a paper, and special sections (appendixes, glossaries, and so on). It is prepared in outline form and may include details about subsections or selected elements.

- *List of illustrations.*   The list of captions that accompany the numbered figures in the paper. Page references are also included.

- *List of tables.*   The list of titles that accompany the numbered tables in the paper. Page references are also included.

- *Preface.*   A section that contextualizes the work: What motivated the study? Under what circumstances did the study begin?

- *Acknowledgments.*   An opportunity for the writer to recognize those who helped with the work—mentors, advisors, colleagues, family members, organizations, sponsors, so on.

- *Editorial method.*   A brief explanation of editorial procedures followed in the paper—for example, regularizing spelling in early print materials, using quotation marks to indicate speeches when none were used in the original text, and so on. These matters may also be addressed in the preface.

- *Abstract.* A brief summative paragraph that articulates the central idea of the study and briefly explains its key elements.

- *Text.* The body of the paper. An informative or persuasive paper contains an introduction, body, and conclusion; it may be divided using headings that describe the main elements of the discussion.

- *Appendixes.* Supplementary information that supports the ideas of the paper but that is awkward to include in the paper itself.

- *Endnotes.* A sequentially numbered list of references that appear in the text of the paper. As an alternative, the same information in the same format can appear at the bottom of pages as footnotes.

- *Glossary.* An alphabetically arranged list of foreign or technical terms, with translations or definitions.

- *Bibliography.* An alphabetical list of sources used in the paper. However, it may also include relevant sources related to the paper that are not cited. (Alternative labels include *Works Cited* and *Literature Cited.*)

States and Territories		
State	*Postal abbreviation*	*Chicago-style abbreviation*
Alabama	AL	Ala.
Alaska	AK	Alaska
American Samoa	AS	American Samoa
Arizona	AZ	Ariz.
Arkansas	AR	Ark.
California	CA	Calif.
Colorado	CO	Colo.
Connecticut	CT	Conn.
Delaware	DE	Del.
District of Columbia	DC	D. C.
Florida	FL	Fla.
Georgia	GA	Ga.
Guam	GU	Guam
Hawaii	HI	Hawaii
Idaho	ID	Idaho
Illinois	IL	Ill.
Indiana	IN	Ind.
Iowa	IA	Iowa
Kansas	KS	Kans.
Kentucky	KY	Ky.
Louisiana	LA	La.
Maine	ME	Maine
Maryland	MD	Md.
Massachusetts	MA	Mass.
Michigan	MI	Mich.
Minnesota	MN	Minn.
Mississippi	MS	Miss.
Missouri	MO	Mo.
Montana	MT	Mont.

State	Postal abbreviation	Chicago-style abbreviation
Nebraska	NE	Neb. *or* Nebr.
Nevada	NV	Nev.
New Hampshire	NH	N.H.
New Jersey	NJ	N.J.
New Mexico	NM	N.Mex.
New York	NY	N.Y.
North Carolina	NC	N.C.
North Dakota	ND	N.Dak.
Ohio	OH	Ohio
Oklahoma	OK	Okla.
Oregon	OR	Ore. *or* Oreg.
Pennsylvania	PA	Pa.
Puerto Rico	PR	P.R. *or* Puerto Rico
Rhode Island	RI	R.I.
South Carolina	SC	S.C.
South Dakota	SD	S.Dak.
Tennessee	TN	Tenn.
Texas	TX	Tex.
Utah	UT	Utah
Vermont	VT	Vt.
Virginia	VA	Va.
Virgin Islands	VI	V.I. *or* Virgin Islands
Washington	WA	Wash.
West Virginia	WV	W.Va.
Wisconsin	WI	Wis. *or* Wisc.
Wyoming	WY	Wyo.

C Sample Pages

ILLUSTRATIONS

Figure		Page
1.	Dutch Colonial House, Hurley, NY	1
2.	French Colonial House, New Orleans, LA	2
3.	Spanish Colonial House, Monterey, CA	3
4.	Georgian House, Philadelphia, PA	3
5.	Adam Townhouse, Easton, MD	4
6.	Early Classical Revival House, Charlottesville, VA	5
7.	Greek Revival House, Milledgeville, GA	5
8.	Gothic Revival House, Tarrytown, NY	6
9.	Italianate House, Portland, ME	7
10.	Second Empire Townhouse, St. Louis, MO	8
11.	Queen Anne House, Chicago, IL	8
12.	Shingle House, Newport, RI	9

TABLES

Table		Page
1.	Population of the American Colonies: 1650, 1700, 1750	2
2.	Centers of Population: 1800, 1850, 1900, 1950, 2000	2
3.	Population by State: 1800, 1850, 1900, 1950, 2000	3
4.	Congressional Apportionments by State: 1800, 1850, 1900, 1950, 2000	4
5.	Ten Largest Cities in the United States: 1800, 1850, 1900, 1950, 2000	5
6.	Largest Metropolitan Areas in the United States: 1800, 1850, 1900, 1950, 2000	5
7.	United States Population by Sex: 1800, 1850, 1900, 1950, 2000	6
8.	United States Population by Median Age: 1800, 1850, 1900, 1950, 2000	7
9.	United States Population of Elderly (65 and over, 85 and over): 1900, 1950, 2000	8
10.	United States Population by Area of Residence (Urban, Rural): 1800, 1850, 1900, 1950, 2000	9

Table 5.   Ten Largest Cities in the United States: 1850, 1900,
            1950, 2000

Rank	City	1850	1900	1950	2000
1.	New York	696,115	3,437,202	7,891,957	8,008,278
2.	Los Angeles	1,610	102,479	1,970,358	3,694,820
3.	Chicago	29,963	1,698,575	3,620,962	2,896,016
4.	Houston	2,396	44,633	596,163	1,953,631
5.	Philadelphia	121,376	1,293,697	2,071,605	1,517,550
6.	Phoenix	. . .	5,544	106,818	1,321,045
7.	San Diego	. . .	17,700	334,387	1,223,400
8.	Dallas	. . .	42,638	434,462	1,188,580
9.	San Antonio	3,488	53,321	408,442	1,144,646
10.	Detroit	21,019	265,704	1,849,568	951,270

Source: United States, Bureau of the Census, Statistical Tables
(2000), http://census.gov/ (accessed April 25, 2006).

GLOSSARY

Balustrade.   A row of small balusters (decorative posts) that support an upper rail.

Bracket.   A feature used for support, usually under eaves. A bracket may be simple or highly decorative.

Cupola.   A small structure built above a roof. A cupola may be small and merely decorative or large enough to enclose a room.

Dormer.   A window set vertically on a sloped roof. A dormer may accommodate only one window or may be wide enough to accommodate a bank of windows.

Eave.   The roof projection that extends beyond the wall of a building. Substantial eaves are often supported by brackets.

Façade.   The vertical face of a structure.

Fanlight.   A half-round window, usually with decorative detail, above a door or a rectangular window.

Gallery.   A wide porch that extends along the entire façade of a building.

Half-timber construction.   A technique by which structural timbers are exposed on the façade, with plaster, brick, or stone between.

Palladian window.   A large window of three parts: the large center window often has an arch; smaller windows appear on either side.

Sample Paper with Footnotes

Plans to construct a memorial to Abraham Lincoln began in March 1867, when the United States Congress established the Lincoln Monument Association; however, the current site for the memorial was not chosen until 1901.[1] Designed by Henry Bacon to resemble a Greek temple, the rectangular Memorial's flat roof is supported by thirty-six columns, one for each state in the Union at the time of Lincoln's death, and texts of Lincoln's Gettysburg Address and second inaugural address are included on the south and north interior walls.[2] The nineteen-foot statue of Lincoln within the Memorial was designed by Daniel Chester French, who later observed, "The memorial tells you what manner of man you are coming to pay homage to: his simplicity, his grandeur, and his power."[3] Jules Guerin, who had done other commissioned work for the government, planned two murals: above the Gettysburg address, a mural was to "[depict] the angel of truth freeing a slave," while above the inaugural speech another mural would represent the unity of the North and South.[4]

With designs complete, construction began on February 12, 1914, forty-nine years after Lincoln's assassination. The exterior was constructed of Colorado Yule marble and Tripods Pink

---

1. United States, National Park Service, "Lincoln Memorial," Monuments and Memorials (1999), http://www.nps.gov/linc/ (accessed March 29, 2006).

2. United States, National Park Service, "Lincoln: The Memorial," Lincoln Memorial (December 22, 2004), http://www.nps.gov/linc/memorial/memorial.htm (accessed April 3, 2006).

3. United States, National Archives and Records Administration, "The Unfinished Lincoln Memorial," National Archives and Records Administration (May 13, 1998), http://www.nara.gov/education/teaching/memorial/memhome.html (accessed April 2, 2006).

4. United States, National Park Service, "Lincoln: The Memorial."

Tennessee marble, while the interior used Indiana limestone and marble from Alabama, Georgia, and Tennessee.[5] Progress was slow, and the Memorial was not completed until early 1922, at a cost of nearly three million dollars.[6] On May 20, 1922, President Warren G. Harding presided over the Memorial's dedication, which included a speech by Robert Morton, President of Tuskegee Institute; in attendance was Robert Todd Lincoln, President Lincoln's son.[7]

In the years that followed, thousands of visitors to the Capital climbed the vast staircase and walked within the Memorial, looking at the mammoth statue of the seated president, reading the carved speeches, and examining the murals. The responses were consistently positive, and the Lincoln Memorial became one of the most popular sites in Washington.

Surely part of the Memorial's appeal is its beauty, but another facet of its appeal rests in the ideals that it represents. Leland M. Roth, in *Understanding Architecture: Its Elements, History, and Meaning,* asserts that the symbolic function of architecture "is most easily perceived in religious and public buildings where the principal intent is to make a broad and emphatic proclamation of communal values and beliefs."[8] In many ways, the Lincoln Memorial does proclaim "values and beliefs." Its size—99 feet high, 188 feet wide, and 118 feet deep—and simple design suggest grandeur and impor-

---

5. United States, National Park Service, "Stones and Mortar: The Statistics of the Monuments and Memorial on the National Mall," National Park Service (January 6, 2004), http://www.nps.gov/mall/mortar/mortar.htm#linc (accessed April 3, 2006).

6. *Encarta Reference,* s.v. "Lincoln Memorial," http://encarta.msn.com/find/concise.asp?ti=0697F000 (accessed March 26, 2006).

7. United States, National Park Service, "Lincoln Memorial."

8. Leland M. Roth, *Understanding Architecture: Its Elements, History, and Meaning* (New York: Icon-Harper, 1993), 5.

tance.[9] Its imposing statue of Lincoln shows a man who was, like the country, strong yet understanding: "One of the president's hands is clenched, representing his strength and determination to see the war to a successful conclusion. The other hand is an open, much more relaxed hand representing his compassionate[,] warm nature."[10] Charles L. Griswold, a professor of philosophy at Boston University, comments on symbolic architecture in this way:

> [T]he architecture by which a people memorializes itself is a species of pedagogy. It therefore seeks to instruct posterity about the past and, in doing so, necessarily reaches a decision about what is worth recovering. . . . We must understand the monument's symbolism, social context, and the effects its architecture works on those who participate in it.[11]

Writing specifically about the Lincoln Memorial, Griswold observes that "Lincoln's temple is, then, a monument to national unity achieved by the martyrdom of Lincoln himself."[12]

Over the years, the Memorial has served a variety of specific ceremonial functions. For example, at noon on February 12 of each year, the current president places a wreath at the side of Lincoln's statue. While most presidents make only brief comments, some see the ceremony as an opportunity to illustrate the symbolic principles of honoring Lincoln, as Harry Truman did in 1947, when the traditional military color guard was made nontraditional and highly symbolic: it was composed of young black children.[13]

---

9. United States, National Park Service, "Stones and Mortar."

10. United States, National Park Service, "Lincoln Memorial."

11. Charles L. Griswold, "The Vietnam Veterans Memorial and the Washington Mall: Philosophical Thoughts on Political Iconography," in *Critical Issues in Public Art: Content, Context, and Controversy,* ed. Harriet F. Senie and Sally Webster (Washington, DC: Smithsonian Institution Press, 1998), 71–73.

12. Ibid., 80.

13. United States, National Archives and Records Administration (May 13, 1998), http://www.nara.gov/cgi-bin/starfinder/ (accessed April 5, 2006).

D Bibliographic Entries

General Principles:
- Separate elements with periods.
- Invert authors' names for alphabetizing.
- Indent second and subsequent lines.
- Provide additional information for added clarity.

BOOKS

5A A BOOK BY ONE AUTHOR

Vachudová, Milada Anna. *Europe Undivided: Democracy, Leverage, and Integration after Communism.* New York: Oxford University Press, 2005.

5B A BOOK BY TWO OR THREE AUTHORS

Downing, John, and Charles Hubbard. *Representing "Race": Racisms, Ethnicities, and Media.* Thousand Oaks, CA: Sage, 2005.

5C A BOOK BY FOUR OR MORE AUTHORS

Tucker, Susan Martin, Mary M. Canobbio, Eleanor Vargo Paquette, and Marjorie Fyfe Wells. *Patient Care Standards: Collaborative Planning and Nursing Interventions.* 7th ed. St. Louis: Mosby-Yearbook, 2000.

Note: All authors' names are listed in the bibliographic entry.

5D A BOOK WITH NO AUTHOR NAMED

An Anglo-Saxon Chronicle. Edited by M. J. Swanton. Exeter, England: University of Exeter Press, 1990.

Note: The abbreviation *ed.* used in the note form is converted to full form in the bibliographic entry.

5E A BOOK BY AN AUTHOR USING A PSEUDONYM

Eliot, George [Mary Ann Evans]. *The Journals of George Eliot.* Edited by Margaret Harris and Judith Johnson. New York: Cambridge University Press, 1998.

Note: Include the author's real name in brackets.

5F A BOOK WITH AN ORGANIZATION AS AUTHOR

American Psychological Association. *Publication Manual of
the American Psychological Association.* 5th ed.
Washington, DC: American Psychological Association,
2001.

5G AN EDITION OTHER THAN THE FIRST

*Forging the American Character: Readings in United States
History.* Edited by John R. M. Wilson. 4th ed. Upper
Saddle River, NJ: Prentice, 2003.

Note: The edition is separated from the title by a period, not
a comma.

5H A REVISED OR ENLARGED EDITION

Wattenburg, Martin P. *The Decline of American Political
Parties: 1952–1996.* Enlarged ed. Cambridge, MA:
Harvard University Press, 1998.

5I A REPRINTED BOOK

Palmer, John. *The Comedy of Manners.* London: Bell, 1913.
Reprinted, New York: Russell, 1962.

Note: The abbreviation used in the note is replaced by the
word.

5J A MULTIVOLUME WORK

American Men and Women of Science. Edited by Pamela M.
Kalte and Katherine H. Nenen. 21st ed. 8 vols. Detroit:
Gale, 2003.

5K AN EDITED COLLECTION

Against the Wall: Israel's Barrier to Peace. Edited by Michael
Sorkin. New York: New Press, 2005.

Note: When an entry is for an entire collection, the title of the
collection and information about the editor are separated by
a period.

5L A SELECTION IN AN EDITED COLLECTION

Jacobs, J. Bruce. "'Taiwanization' in Taiwan's Politics." In
Cultural, Ethnic, and Political Nationalism in

Contemporary Taiwan, edited by John Makeham and A-Chin Hsiau, 17–54. New York: Palgrave, 2005.

Note: When an entry describes a selection in a collection, the information about the editor of the collection is separated from the collection's title by a comma, not a period; inclusive page numbers are separated from the editor's name by a comma.

5M MULTIPLE REFERENCES TO THE SAME COLLECTION

The China Threat: Perceptions, Myths, and Reality. Edited by Herbert Yee and Ian Storey. London: Routledge, 2002.

Kim, Taeho. "South Korea and a Rising China: Perceptions, Policies, and Prospects." In *The China Threat,* 166–80.

Sukma, Rizal. "Indonesia's Perceptions of China: The Domestic Bases of Persistent Ambiguity." In *The China Threat,* 181–204.

Note: The collection must have a separately prepared bibliographic entry.

5N AN ARTICLE IN AN ENCYCLOPEDIA OR OTHER REFERENCE WORK

Abrams, Richard M. "Theodore Roosevelt." In *The Presidents: A Reference History.* Edited by Henry F. Graff. 2nd ed. New York: Scribner's, 1996.

Note: Well-known reference sources (major encyclopedias, fact books, and so on) are listed in reference notes; they do not have to be included in a bibliography.

5O A WORK IN A SERIES

Fogg, B. J. *Persuasive Technology: Using Computers to Change What We Think and Do.* Interactive Technology Series. Boston: Kaufman, 2003.

5P AN IMPRINT

Adetago, Adetayo. *Telling Our Stories: Continuities and Divergencies in Black Autobiography.* New York: Macmillan, Palgrave, 2005.

5Q A TRANSLATION

Arjeu, Mulder. *Understanding Media Theory: Language,
Image, Sound, Behavior.* Translated by Laura Martz.
New York: Distributed Art, 2004.

5R A GOVERNMENT DOCUMENT— *CONGRESSIONAL RECORD*

Introduction of the Campaign Spending Limit and Election
Reform Act of 1993. *Congressional Record* 139 (June 15,
1993): 7276.

5S A GOVERNMENT DOCUMENT— COMMITTEE, COMMISSION, DEPARTMENT

U.S. Congress. Budget Office. *Budget of the United States
Government, Fiscal Year 2002.* Washington, DC: GPO,
2003.

5T A PREFACE, INTRODUCTION, FOREWORD, EPILOGUE, OR AFTERWORD

Elam, Harry J., Jr. "(W)righting History: A Meditation in Four
Beats." Introduction to *The Past and Present in the
Drama of August Wilson.* Ann Arbor: University of
Michigan Press, 2004.

Note: Inclusive page numbers are not required for front or
back matter.

5U PAMPHLET OR BROCHURE

Wyatt, Mike. *Taking Off: A Guide to Backpacking Trails
across North America.* Emmaus, PA: Rodale,
1990.

5V PUBLISHED PROCEEDINGS FROM A CONFERENCE

Rich, John A. "The Health Crisis of Young Black Men in the
Inner City." In *The Crisis of the Young African American
Male in the Inner City.* United States Commission on
Civil Rights, April 15–16, 1999. Washington, DC: GPO,
2000.

5w A Dissertation

Parnet, Harriet L. "The Terror of Our Days: Four American
Poets Respond to the Holocaust." PhD diss., Lehigh
University, 2000.

5x A Book Written in a Language Other than English

Genet, Jean. *Les bonnes* [The Maids]. In *Oeuvres complètes*
[Complete Works]. Paris: Gallimard, 1968.

5y Sacred Writings

The Bhagavad Gita. Translated by Juan Mascaró. New York:
Penguin Books, 1962.

Note: Standard versions of sacred writings are cited in
reference notes; they may then be ommited from a
bibliography.

5z A Secondary Source

Goodwin, Doris Kearns. *Team of Rivals: The Political Genius
of Abraham Lincoln.* New York: Simon, 2005.
Stoddard, William O. *Dispatches from Lincoln's White House:
The Anonymous Civil War Journalism of Presidential
Secretary William O. Stoddard.* Edited by Michael
Burlingame. Lincoln: University of Nebraska Press,
2002.

Note: Both the primary and secondary source must appear
in the bibliography.

PERIODICALS

6a An Article in a Journal with Continuous Paging

Bick, Sally. "*Of Mice and Men:* Copland, Hollywood, and
American Musical Modernism." *American Music* 23
(2005): 426–72.

Note: Bibliographic entries require inclusive page numbers
for articles.

6B AN ARTICLE IN A JOURNAL WITH SEPARATE PAGING

Barrett, Wayne. "G. F. Handel's *Messiah:* Drama Theolicus: A Discussion of *Messiah's* Text with Implications for Its Performance." *Choral Journal* 46, no. 6 (2005): 8–14.

6C AN ARTICLE IN A MONTHLY MAGAZINE

Koplos, Janet. "Portraits of Light." *Art in America,* February 2006, 82–89.

6D AN ARTICLE IN A WEEKLY MAGAZINE

Malcolm, Janet. "The Art of Testifying: The Confirmation Hearings as Theatre." *New Yorker,* March 13, 2006, 70–79.

6E AN ARTICLE IN A NEWSPAPER

Davis, Francis. "Strata Various." *Village Voice,* March 8–14, 2006.

Note: Newspaper articles are listed in reference notes; they do not have to be included in a bibliography.

6F AN EDITORIAL OR A LETTER TO THE EDITOR

Will, George F. "Professors of Pretense." Editorial. *Washington Post,* March 8, 2006.

6G A REVIEW

Guerra, Gustavo. Review of *Pragmatism, Postmodernism, and the Future of Philosophy,* by John J. Stuhr. *Journal of Speculative Philosophy* 19 (2005): 274–76.

6H AN ABSTRACT FROM *DISSERTATION ABSTRACTS INTERNATIONAL*

Dikovitskaya, Margarita. "From Art to Visual Culture: The Study of the Visual after the Cultural Turn." PhD diss., Columbia University. *Dissertation Abstracts International* 62 (2002), AAT3028516.

6i   A Secondary Source

Druckman, James N., and Michael Perkin. "The Impact of Media Bias: How Editorial Slant Effects Voters." *Journal of Politics* 67 (2005): 1030–49.

McGraw, Kathleen M. "Political Impressions." In *Political Psychology,* edited by David O. Sears, Leonie Huddy, and Robert Jervis, 394–432. Oxford: Oxford University Press, 2003.

AUDIOVISUAL

7a   A Film

Lee, Ang, dir. *Brokeback Mountain.* With Heath Ledger, Jake Gyllenhaal, and Michelle Williams. Los Angeles, CA: Focus Features, River Road Entertainment, 2005. Film.

7b   A Filmstrip

The Great American Deficit: Mortgaging the Future. Current Affairs Series. New York: Contemporary Media, New York Times, 1986. Filmstrip.

7c   A Television Broadcast

Empire Falls. With Ed Harris, Helen Hunt, Joanne Woodward, Paul Newman, Robin Wright Penn, Aidan Quinn, and Philip Seymour Hoffman. HBO, May 5, 2005.

7d   A Radio Broadcast

"The War of the Worlds." With Orson Welles. WCBS, October 30, 1938.

7e   A Recording

The Beatles. *Abbey Road.* Compact disc. Capital-EMI CDp7-46446-2, 1969.

7f   A Performance

Long Day's Journey into Night. Written by Eugene O'Neill. With Vanessa Redgrave, Brian Dennehy, Robert Sean Leonard, and Philip Seymour Hoffman. Plymouth Theatre, New York, August 17, 2003.

7G AN INTERVIEW

Otwell, Stephen. Interview by author. Cook County Library, Chicago, February 14, 2006.

7H A TRANSCRIPT

Koch, Kathleen. *Saving My Town: The Fight for Bay St. Louis.* Transcript. C*NN Presents.* CNN, February 26, 2006.

7I A LECTURE OR SPEECH

Bebbington, Paul. "Who's the Greatest? Minds That Changed Our Minds." Lecture, Royal Institution, London, April 27, 2006.

7J A WORK OF ART

Gauguin, Paul. *The Brooding Woman.* Oil on canvas, 1891. Worcester Art Museum, Worcester, MA.

7K AN EXHIBIT

"Life in the Shadows: Hidden Children and the Holocaust." Exhibit. Museum of Jewish Heritage, New York, May 1, 2006.

7L A MAP, GRAPH, TABLE, OR CHART

Weighty Matters. Graph. "The Politics of Fat," by Karen Tumulty. *Time,* March 27, 2006, 42.

7M A CARTOON

Bek. "I don't know if he's a great artist, but he's certainly annoying." Cartoon. *New Yorker,* August 11, 2003, 60.

ELECTRONIC

8A AN ONLINE SCHOLARLY PROJECT, INFORMATION DATABASE, OR PROFESSIONAL WEB SITE

The On-line Books Page. Edited by John Mark Ockerbloom. Philadelphia: University of Pennsylvania, 2006. http://digital.library.upenn.edu/books (accessed March 15, 2006).

8B A SOURCE FROM AN ONLINE SCHOLARLY PROJECT, INFORMATION DATABASE, OR PROFESSIONAL WEB SITE

Roosevelt, Franklin. "A Date Which Will Live in Infamy": Joint Address to Congress. Speech, U. S. Congress, Washington, DC, December 8, 1941. America's Historical Documents. National Archives and Record Administration. College Park, MD: NARA, 2005. http://www.archives.gov/historical-docs/ (accessed April 3, 2006).

8C AN ONLINE BOOK

Lofting, Hugh. *The Voyages of Doctor Dolittle.* Philadelphia: Lippincott, 1922. Project Gutenberg. Urbana: University of Illinois, 1998. http://www.Gutenberg .org/dirs/etext98/vdrdl10.txt (accessed February 24, 2006).

8D AN ARTICLE IN AN ONLINE JOURNAL

Willer, Robb. "The Effects of Government-Issued Terror Warnings on Presidential Approval Ratings." *Current Research in Social Psychology* 10, no. 1 (2004). http://www.uiowa.edu/%7Egrpproc/crisp/prior .html (accessed April 6, 2006).

8E AN ARTICLE IN AN ONLINE MAGAZINE

Stewart, Doug. "Resurrecting Pompeii." *Smithsonian,* February 2006. http://www.smithsonianmagazine .com/issues/2006/February/Pompeii.php?page=1 (accessed March 22, 2006).

8F AN ARTICLE IN AN ONLINE NEWSPAPER

O'Connor, Phillip, and Eun Kyung Kim. "Illegal Workers: Gain or Drain?" *St. Louis Post Dispatch,* April 1, 2006. http://www.stltoday.com/stltoday/news/ stories/nsf/stlouiscitycounty/story/ 30333179F95C576B2862571430075A5FF? OpenDocument (accessed April 3, 2006).

8G AN ARTICLE IN AN ONLINE ENCYCLOPEDIA OR OTHER REFERENCE SOURCE

Infoplease Almanac. S.V. "Children in Foster Care."
    http://www.infoplease.com/ipa/A0778809.html
    (accessed March 22, 2006).

Note: Although reference sources are included in notes, they do not have to be included in the bibliography.

8H AN ONLINE GOVERNMENT DOCUMENT

U.S. Congress. Budget Office. *Immigration Policy in the United States.,* Congressional Budget Office. Washington, DC: GPO, February 2006. http://www.cbo.gov/ftpdocs/70xx/doc7051/ 02-28-Immigration.pdf (accessed March 6, 2006).

8I AN ONLINE TRANSCRIPT OF A LECTURE OR SPEECH

Faulkner, William. Nobel Prize in Literature Acceptance. Speech, Nobel Prize Ceremony, Stockholm, December 10, 1950. http://www.historyplace.com/speeches/ faulkner.htm (accessed February 1, 2006).

8J AN ONLINE WORK OF ART

Wood, Grant. *American Gothic.* Oil on beaverboard, 1930. Art Institute of Chicago. http://www.artic.edu/aic/ collections/american/highlight_item?acc=1930.934& page=16 (accessed January 20, 2006).

8K AN ONLINE EXHIBIT

"Cover Art: The *Time* Collection at the National Portrait Gallery." Exhibit. National Portrait Gallery, Washington, DC, December 2005. http://www.npg .si.edu/time/ (accessed April 2, 2006).

8L AN ONLINE MAP, GRAPH, TABLE, OR CHART

Families in Poverty by Size of Family and Number of Related Children: 2004. Table. Current Population Survey. 2005 Annual Social and Economic Supplement. Washington, DC: U.S. Census Bureau, 2005. http:// pubdb3.census.gov/macro/032005/new37_000.htm (accessed April 8, 2006).

8M AN ONLINE TRANSCRIPT OF A TELEVISION OR RADIO BROADCAST

"Supreme Ethics Problem." *Nightline.* With Cynthia
McFadden. ABC, January 23, 2006. http://abcnews
.go.com/Nightline/story?id=1541642 (accessed
March 12, 2006).

8N AN ONLINE AUDIO SOURCE

"Martin Luther King Delivers 'I Have a Dream' Speech."
Audio recording. This Day in History, August 28, 1963.
http://www.historychannel.com/broadband/
clipview/index.jsp?id=tdih_0828.54seconds
(accessed March 29, 2006).

8O A CD-ROM SOURCE

Spafford, Carol Sullivan, Augustus J. Itzo Pesce, and George
S. Grosser. *Education Dictionary.* CD-ROM. Florence,
KY: Delmar Learning, 2006.

8P AN E-MAIL INTERVIEW

Washburne-Freise, Marla. E-mail interview by author,
May 14, 2006.

Note: Although personal communication is included in
notes, it does not have to be included in a bibliography.

8Q AN ONLINE POSTING

"Threatened and Endangered Species Recovery Act."
Native Plants Forum, October 3, 2005. http://
forums.gardenweb.com/forums/load/natives/
msg1013431130746.html?26 (accessed January 14,
2006).

Index

Abbreviations
  et al. ("and others"), 78
  for note-taking, 14
  and note forms, 64
  of states, 129–130
  of territories, 129–130
Abstracts
  bibliographic entries for, 141
  in *Dissertation Abstracts International*, 92
  as elements of papers, 128
  periodical databases and, 8
Access statements (online sources), 106
Acknowledgements, as elements of papers, 127
Afterwords
  bibliographic entries for, 139
  note forms for, 85
Agreement
  editorial style and, 55–57
  pronoun-antecedent, 56–57
  subject-verb, 56
Alphabetizing bibliographies, 68–69
Ampersands (&), 68
Annotated bibliographies
  continuous style, 71
  paragraph style, 71
Appendixes
  elements of, 32
  as elements of papers, 26, 128
  format for, 32
Argumentative papers
  elements of, 31
  organization of, 31
  sample of, 111–126
Art, works of
  bibliographic entries for, 143
  note forms for, 98–99
  and source evaluation, 10
Art, works of (online)
  bibliographic entries for, 145
  note forms for, 107

Articles
  citation-abstract, 8
  full-text, 8
  page image, 8
  in periodical databases, 7–8
Articles, note forms for, *see*
    Electronic sources;
    Periodicals
Audio sources (online)
  bibliographic entries for, 146
  note forms for, 109
Audiovisual sources (note forms), **7**:
  art, works of, 98–99
  broadcasts (radio), 96
  broadcasts (television), 95
  cartoons, 100
  charts, 99
  exhibits, 99
  films, 94–95
  filmstrips, 95
  graphs, 99
  interviews, 97
  lectures, 98
  maps, 99
  performances, 97
  recordings, 96–97
  slide programs, 95
  source evaluation and, 10
  speeches, 98
  tables, 99
  transcripts, 98
  see also Bibliographic entries;
    Electronic sources; Evaluation; Note forms
Authorless sources
  bibliographic entries for, 136
  and bibliographies, 69
  note forms for, 79
Authors
  bibliographies and, 68
  credentials, 9
  and Internet sources, 103, 105, 106, 109, 110
  names (for note-taking), 14
  and online catalogs, 6

Authors (*cont.*)
   and periodical databases, 7
   using pseudonyms, 70, 79,
      136
   note forms and, 63, 65
   and source evaluation, 9, 11,
      12
   using pseudonyms, 70

Biased language
   gender, 60–61
   other forms, 61
   racial and ethnic, 59–60
Bibliographic entries
   abstracts from *Dissertation
      Abstracts International*, 141,
   afterwords, 139
   art, works of, 143
   art, works of (online), 145
   audio source (online), 146
   authorless sources, 136
   books by four or more
      authors, 136
   books by one author, 136
   books by two or three
      authors, 136
   books in a language other
      than English, 140
   books (online), 144
   books with an author (pseu-
      donym), 136
   books with an organization
      as author, 137
   books with no author
      named, 136
   broadcasts (radio), 142
   broadcasts (radio), tran-
      scripts of (online), 146
   broadcasts (television), 142
   broadcasts (television), tran-
      scripts of (online), 146
   brochures, 139
   cartoons, 143
   CD-ROM sources, 146
   charts, 143
   charts (online), 145
   cities (of publication), 64
   collections, works in, 137–138
   dissertations, 140

edited collections, 137
editions other than first, 137
editorials, 141
encyclopedias, articles in, 138
encyclopedias (online), articles in, 145
enlarged editions, 137
epilogues, 139
exhibits, 143
exhibits (online), 145
films, 142
filmstrips, 142
forewords, 139
government documents, 139
government documents (*Congressional Record*), 139
government documents
   (online), 145
graphs, 143
graphs (online), 145
imprints, 138
information databases
   (online), 143
interviews, 143
interviews, e-mail, 146
introductions, 139
journals (continuous pag-
   ing), articles in, 140
journals (online), articles in,
   144
journals (separate paging),
   articles in, 141
lectures, 143
lectures, transcripts of
   (online), 145
letters to the editor, 141
magazines (monthly), articles in, 141
magazines (online), articles
   in, 144
magazines (weekly), articles
   in, 141
maps, 143
maps (online), 145
multiple references (to the
   same collection), 138
multivolume works, 137
newspapers, articles in, 141
newspapers (online), articles
   in, 144

pamphlets, 139
performances, 142
postings (online), 146
prefaces, 139
primary sources, 88
proceedings (from a conference), 139
recordings, 142
reference works, articles in, 138
reference works (online), articles in, 145
reprinted books, 137
reviews, 141
revised editions, 137
sacred writings, 140
scholarly projects (online), 143
secondary sources, 140, 142
selections in an edited collection, 137–138
series, works in a, 138
slide programs, 142
speeches, 143
speeches, transcripts of (online), 145
tables, 143
tables (online), 145
transcripts, 143
translations, 139
Web sites (professional), 143
see also Note forms
Bibliographies, **4h-41:**
alphabetizing, 68–69
annotated, 71
authors using pseudonyms, 70
elements of, 67–68
as elements of papers, 26, 31, 34, 128
format for, 68
four or more authors (editors), 70
information for, 67–68
multiple works by same author, 69, 125–126
revision and, 24
in sample papers, 124–126
samples (of individual entries), 136–146

Block quotations (long), 73
Books (note forms for), **5:**
afterwords in, 85
with an author (pseudonym), 79
dissertations, 86–87
edited collections, 81
editions other than the first, 80
encyclopedias, articles in, 82
enlarged editions, 80
epilogues in, 85
forewords in, 85
by four or more authors, 78–79
government documents as, 84–85
government documents (*Congressional Record*), 84
imprints, 83
introductions in, 85
in a language other than English, 87
multivolume, 81
with no authors named, 70
by one author, 78
online, 104
with organizations as authors, 79
pamphlets, 86
prefaces in, 85
primary sources, 88
proceedings (from a conference), 86
reference works, articles in, 82
reprinted, 80
revised editions, 80
sacred writings, 87
secondary sources, 88
selections in edited collections, 81
in a series, 82
titles and note forms, 63
translations, 83–84
by two or three authors, 78
see also Bibliographic entries; Electronic sources; Evaluation; Note forms; Separately published materials

Brackets
    with quotations, 75
    uses of, 44
Broadcasts (radio)
    bibliographic entries for, 142
    note forms for, 96
    and source evaluation, 10
Broadcasts (radio), transcripts
        of (online)
    bibliographic entries for, 146
    note forms for, 108–109
Broadcasts (television)
    bibliographic entries for, 142
    note forms for, 95
    and source evaluation, 10
Broadcasts (television), tran-
        scripts of (online)
    bibliographic entries for 146,
    note forms for, 108–109
Brochures
    bibliographic entries for, 139
    note forms for, 86

Call numbers, online catalogs
        and, 7
Capitalization
    headline style, 46
    no use of, 48
    note forms and, 65
    sentence style, 46
    title pages and, 25
    of titles, 47
    uses of, 46–48
Card catalogs, *see* Online cata-
        logs
Cartoons,
    bibliographic entries for, 143
    note forms for, 100
Catalogs (computer), 5
Categories (for note-taking), 14
CD-ROM sources
    bibliographic entries for, 146
    limited use of, 109
    note forms for, 109
Charts
    bibliographic entries for, 143
    note forms for, 99
    and source evaluation, 10
Charts (online)

bibliographic entries for, 145
    note forms for, 108
Citations
    and abstracts, 8
    periodical databases and, 7–8
Citations, *see* Note forms
Cities (of publication)
    and bibliographic entries, 64
    and online catalogs, 7
    and periodical databases, 7
    and note forms, 64
Classification, by subject, (in
        online catalogs), 7
Collections, edited,
    bibliographic entries for,
        137–138
    note forms for, 81
Collections, works in
    bibliographic entires for,
        137–138
    note forms for, 81
Colloquialisms, 58–59
Colons, uses of, 40–41
Combinations (of sources),
        12–13
Commas, uses of, 39–40
Common knowledge, 16–17
Compilers, and note forms, 64
Computers
    for creating figures, 28
    for note-taking, 13
Conclusions
    as elements of papers, 31
    in sample paper, 119–120
    writing and, 23
Content
    drafting, 21, 22
    revision and, 23
Copyright pages, 64
Countries (of publication), 64
Course-related research goals,
        3–4
Current periodicals, in li-
        braries, 5

Dashes, uses of, 42–43
Dates (of publication)
    and periodical databases, 7
    and note forms, 64

Dedications, as elements of papers, 127
Diction, *see* Word choice
Disk copies (of manuscripts), 37
Dissertations
    bibliographic entries for, 140
    note forms for, 86–87
Dissertation Abstracts International
    bibliographic entries for, 141
    note forms for, 92
Domains (in Internet addresses), 11
Drafts (of research papers), 21–23

Edited collections
    bibliographic entries for, 137
    note forms for, 81
Editions
    bibliographic entries for, 137
    enlarged, 80
    and online catalogs, 7
    other than first, 80
    and note forms, 64
    note forms for, 80
    revised, 80
Editor, letters to the
    bibliographic forms for, 141
    note forms for, 92
Editorial methods, explanation of, as elements of papers, 127
Editors, and note forms, 63, 64
Editorial style, *see* individual elements
Editorials
    bibliographic entries for, 141
    note forms for, 92
Electronic addresses (URLs), 8, 11, 102
Electronic search systems, *see* Online catalogs
Electronic sources (note forms), **8**:
    art, works of (online), 107
    audio sources (online), 109
    books (online), 104
broadcasts (radio), transcript (online), 108–109
broadcasts (television), transcript (online), 108–109
CD-ROM sources, 109
charts (online), 108
encyclopedias (online), articles in, 106
exhibits (online), 108
government documents (online), 106–107
graphs (online), 108
information databases, 102–103
interviews, e-mail, 109
journals (online), articles in, 104–105
lectures, transcripts of (online), 107
magazines (online), articles in, 105
maps (online), 108
newspapers (online), articles in, 105–106
postings (online), 110
professional Web sites, 102, 103
reference works (online), articles in, 106
scholarly projects, 102, 103
sources (from scholarly projects, information databases, or professional Web sites), 103
specialized sources (scholarly project, information database, or professional Web site), 102, 103
speeches, transcripts of (online), 107
tables (online), 108
Web sites (professional), 102–103
see also Bibliographic entries; Evaluation; Note forms
Ellipsis points
    with quotations, 76
    uses of, 45–46
E-mail, *see* Interviews

Encyclopedias, articles in
  bibliographic entries for, 138
  note forms for, 82
Encyclopedias (online), articles
    in
  bibliographic entries for, 145
  note forms for, 106
Endnotes
  elements of, 63–65
  as elements of paper, 26, 31,
      32–33, 128
  format for, 33, 65
  information for, 63–64
  placement of, 33, 62–63
  positioning, 66
  punctuation with, 33, 66
  revision and, 24
  in sample paper, 121–123
  writing and, 23
  see also Note forms
Enlarged editions
  bibliographic entries for, 137
  note forms for, 80
Entry forms, *see* Note forms
Epigraphs, as elements of
      papers, 127
Epilogues
  bibliographic entries for, 139
  note forms for, 85
et al. ("and others"), 78
Ethnic bias (word choice),
      59–60
Evaluation (of sources), **1e**:
  audiovisual sources, 10
  and combinations of
      sources, 12–13
  of Internet (electronic)
      sources, 10–12
  of print sources, 9–10
Exclamation points, uses of, 42
Exhibits
  bibliographic entries for, 143
  note forms for, 99
Exhibits (online)
  bibliographic entries for, 145
  note forms for, 108

Facts (and note-taking), 14
Facts of publication

  and online catalogs, 7
  and note forms, 64
Figure captions
  credit lines for, 28
  elements of, 27
  format for, 27–28
  in sample paper, 114, 118
Figures
  computer-generated, 28
  concerns about using,
      28–29
  elements of, 27–28
  as elements of papers, 26
  format for, 27–28
  list of (illustrations), 26, 27
  placement of, 27
  in sample paper, 114, 118
  value of, 28
  visual clutter and, 28–29
Films
  bibliographic entries, 142
  note forms for, 94–95
  and source evaluation, 10
Filmstrips
  bibliographic entries for,
      142
  note forms for, 95
Fonts
  italics for, 34
  serif, 34
Footnotes
  elements of, 62, 63–65
  as elements of papers, 62, 66,
      133–135
  format for, 65
  information for, 63–64
  placement of, 62–63
  positioning, 66
  punctuation with, 33, 63
  revision and, 24
  writing and, 23
  see also Note forms
Forewords
  bibliographic entries for, 139
  note forms for, 85
Format
  for bibliographic entries, 68
  for note forms, 65
  for note-taking, 14
Full-text articles, 8

Gender bias (word choice), 60–61
Glossaries
 arrangement of, 33–34
 as elements of papers, 26, 128
 format for, 34
 sample, 132
Goals, research, *see* Research goals
Government documents
 bibliographic entries for, 139
 area, in library, 5
 note forms for, 84–85
Government documents (*Congressional Record*)
 bibliographic entries for, 139
 note forms for, 84
Government documents (online)
 bibliographic entries for, 142
 note forms for, 106
Grammar, revision and, 24
Graphs
 bibliographic entries for, 143
 note forms for, 99
 and source evaluation, 10
Graphs (online)
 bibliographic entries for, 145
 note forms for, 108

Headings
 levels of, 36
 for manuscript sections, 27, 29, 32, 33
 revision and, 23
Headline-style capitalization, 46
Home pages, *see* Web sites
Hyphens, uses of, 42
Hypotheses
 definition of, 3
 revision and, 23
 writing and, 22

Ibid ("in the same place"), 66
Illustrations, see Figures
Illustrations, lists of
 as elements of papers, 26, 127
 format for, 27
 sample, 131

Imprints
 bibliographic entries for, 138
 note form for, 83
Indentations
 and bibliographic entries, 68
 for long quotations, 73, 74
 in manuscripts, 35
 and note forms, 65
Indirect sources, *see* Secondary sources
Information databases (online)
 bibliographic entries for, 143
 definition of, 102
 note forms for, 102, 103
Internet sources
 and electronic addresses, 8
 and information databases, 102
 and research methods, 8–9
 and scholarly projects, 102
 and source evaluation, 10–12
 and Web sites, 102
 see also Electronic sources; Evaluation
Interviews
 bibliographic entries for, 143
 note forms for, 97
Interviews, e-mail
 bibliographic entries for, 146
 note forms for, 109
Introductions
 bibliographic entries for, 139
 as element of papers, 31
 note forms for, 85
 in sample paper, 111–112
 writing and, 23
Issue numbers
 and periodical databases, 7
 and note forms, 90
Italics
 and manuscripts, 34, 48–49
 with titles, 48
 uses of, 48–49

Jargon, 58
Journals (continuous paging), articles in
 bibliographic entries for, 140

Journals (continuous paging),
  articles in (*cont.*)
  note forms for, 89–90
  and source evaluation, 10
Journals (online), articles in
  bibliographic entries for, 144
  note forms for, 104–105
Journals (separate paging),
  articles in
  bibliographic entries for, 141
  note forms for, 90
  and source evaluation, 10

Keyword searching, 6

Lectures
  bibliographic entries for, 143
  note forms for, 98
  and source evaluation, 10
Lectures, transcripts of (online)
  bibliographic entries for, 145
  note forms for, 107
Letters to the editor
  bibliographic entries for, 141
  note forms for, 92
Levels (of headings), *see*
  Headings
Libraries
  research areas in, 5–6
  research based in, 5–6
  special, 6
Line spacing
  and appendixes, 32
  and bibliographic entries, 68
  double spacing, 35
  and endnotes, 33, 65
  and footnotes 65
  glossary, 34
  and list of illustrations, 27
  and list of tables, 29
  for long quotations, 73
  and note forms, 65
Lists of illustrations
  as elements of papers, 26, 127
  format for, 27
  sample, 131
Lists of tables
  as elements of papers, 26, 127
  format for, 29
  sample, 131

Magazines (monthly), articles in
  bibliographic entries for, 141
  note forms for, 91
  and source evaluation, 10
Magazines (online), articles in
  bibliographic entries for, 144
  note forms for, 105
Magazine (weekly), articles in
  bibliographic entries for, 141
  note forms for, 91
  and source evaluation, 10
Manuscript guidelines, **2b**:
  appendixes, 32
  argumentative papers, 31
  bibliographies, 34
  endnotes, 32–33
  figure captions, 28
  figures, 27–29
  font selection, 34
  footnotes, 32
  glossaries, 33–34
  headings (for sections), 36
  indentations, 35
  line spacing, 35
  lists of illustrations, 27–29
  lists of tables, 29
  margins, 35
  order of, 37
  paging, 35
  paper (for printing), 34
  papers (kinds of), 34
  parts of papers, 26
  reviews, 31
  revision and, 24
  for submitting papers, 36–37
  tables, 30–31
  text (of the paper), 31
  title pages, 25, 26
  titles, 25, 31, 36
Maps
  bibliographic entries for, 143
  note forms for, 99
  and source evaluation, 10
Maps (online)
  bibliographic entries for, 145
  note forms for, 108
Margins, 35
Mechanics
  capitalization, 46–48
  italics, 48–49

number style, 49–53
revision and, 24
Media area, in library, 6
Microforms area, in library, 6
Motion pictures, see Films
Multiple notes (same collection)
  bibliographic entries for, 138
  note forms for, 66–67
Multiple references (in the same note), 67
Multiple works (same author), in bibliography, 68, 70
Multivolume works
  bibliographic entries for, 137
  note forms for, 81

New books area, in library, 6
Newspapers, articles in
  bibliographic entries for, 141
  note forms for, 91
  and source evaluation, 10
Newspapers (online), articles in
  bibliographic entries for, 144
  note forms for, 105–106
Note cards (for note-taking), 13
Note forms
  abbreviations and, 38, 64
  abstracts, from *Dissertation Abstracts International*, 92
  afterwords, 85
  art, works of, 98–99
  art, works of (online), 107
  audio sources (online), 109
  authorless sources, 79
  authors, 63
  books by four or more authors, 78–79
  books by one author, 78
  books by two or more authors, 78
  books in a language other than English, 87
  books (online), 104
  books with an author (pseudonym), 79
  books with an organization as author, 79

books with no author named, 79
broadcasts (radio), 96
broadcasts (radio), transcripts of (online), 108–109
broadcasts (television), 95
broadcasts (television), transcripts of (online), 108–109
brochures, 86
capitalization (of titles), 47
cartoons, 100
CD-ROM sources, 109
charts, 99
charts (online), 108
cities (of publication), 64
collections, edited, 81
collections, works in, 81
countries (of publication), 65
dates (of publication), 65
dissertations, 86–87
edited collections, 81
editions other than first, 64, 80
editorials, 92
editors, 64
encyclopedias, articles in, 82
encyclopedias (online), articles in, 106
enlarged editions, 80
epilogues, 85
exhibits, 99
exhibits (online), 108
facts of publications, 64
films, 94–95
filmstrips, 95
forewords, 85
government documents, 84–85
government documents (*Congressional Record*), 84
government documents (online), 106–107
graphs, 99
graphs (online), 108
indentation and, 65
information databases (online), 103
information for, 63–65

Note forms (*cont.*)
  imprint, 83
  interviews, 97
  interviews, e-mail, 109
  introductions, 85
  issue numbers, 64, 90
  italics with titles, 65
  journals (continuous pag-
    ing), articles in, 89–90
  journals (online), articles in,
    104–105
  journals (separate paging),
    articles in, 90
  lectures, 98
  lectures, transcripts of (on-
    line), 107
  letters to the editor, 92
  line spacing and, 65
  magazines (monthly), arti-
    cles in, 91
  magazines (online), articles
    in, 105
  magazines (weekly), articles
    in, 91
  maps, 99
  maps (online), 108
  multiple notes (same
    source), 66–67
  multiple references (in the
    same note), 67, 82
  multivolume works, 81
  newspapers, articles in, 91
  newspapers (online), articles
    in, 105–106
  organizations as author, 79
  page numbers and, 64
  pamphlets, 86
  performances, 97
  postings (online), 110
  prefaces, 85
  primary sources, 88, 93
  proceedings (from a confer-
    ence), 86
  publication dates, 64
  publishers, 64–65
  punctuation (of titles), 65
  punctuation (within notes),
    65
  recordings, 96–97
  reference works, articles in, 82

  reference works (online), ar-
    ticles in, 106
  reprinted books, 80
  retrieval statements, 106
  reviews, 92
  revised editions, 80
  sacred writings, 87
  scholarly projects (online),
    103
  secondary sources, 88, 93
  selections in edited collec-
    tions, 81
  series, works in a, 64, 82
  slide programs, 95
  spacing within notes, 65
  speeches, 98
  speeches, transcripts of (on-
    line), 107
  tables, 99
  tables (online), 108
  titles, 63, 65
  transcripts, 98
  translations, 83–84
  translators, 64
  URLs, 8, 11, 102
  volume numbers, 64, 90
  Web sites (professional), 103
  works in collections, 81
  see also Bibliographic entries
Notes
  planning and, 20
  writing and, 22
Note numbers
  placement of, 33, 62, 63
  punctuation with, 33, 63
Note-taking, **1f**:
  approaches to, 13
  and facts, 14
  format for, 14
  information for, 13–14
  kinds of notes for, 14–15
  and paraphrases, 15
  and plagiarism, 17–19
  and quotations, 15
  methods for, 13
  and summaries, 14–15
Noun clusters, 58
Number style
  cardinal numbers, 52
  commas in numbers, 52

inclusive numbers, 53
using numerals, 51–52
ordinal numbers, 52
plurals of numbers, 52
uses of, 49–53
using words for numbers, 50

Objectives (stated)
definition of, 3
elements of, 3
planning and, 20
writing and, 20, 22
Online catalogs
and authors, 6
and call numbers, 7
and editions, 7
and facts of publication, 7
and location (in library), 5, 7
and notes, 7
and numbers of items, 7
and research methods, 6–7
and status (checkout), 7
and subject classifications, 7
and table of contents, 7
and technical descriptions, 7
and titles, 6
Online sources, *see* Electronic
sources; individual types
of sources
Organization
drafting and, 22
revision and, 23
Organizations, as authors, 79
Outlines
conventions for, 20–21
formal, 20–21
informal, 20
planning and, 20–21
writing and, 22

Paging (manuscript), 35
Pamphlets
bibliographic entries for, 139
note forms for, 86
Page numbers
for note-taking, 14
and note forms, 64
Page-image articles, 8

Paper
for final manuscripts, 34
for note-taking, 13
Paper, sample, *see* Sample paper
Parallelism, editorial style and,
57
Paraphrases (and note-taking),
15
Parentheses, uses of, 43
Performances
bibliographic entries for, 142
note forms for, 97
Periodical databases
and article titles, 7
and authors, 7
and citation-abstracts,
and cities, 7
and dates, 7
and formats (for articles), 8
and full-text articles, 8
and issue numbers, 7
and numbers of pages, 8
and page-image articles,
and periodical titles, 7
and research methods, 6–9
and start pages, 7
and volume numbers, 7
Periodicals
current area, in library, 5
and source evaluations, 10
Periodicals (note forms), **6**:
abstracts from *Dissertation
Abstracts International*, 92
editorials, 92
issue numbers and note
forms, 90
journals (continuous pag-
ing), articles in, 89–90
journal (separate paging), articles in, 90
letters to the editor, 92
magazines (monthly), articles in, 91
magazines (weekly), articles
in, 91
newspapers, articles in, 91
pages,
primary sources, 93
reviews, 92

Periodicals (note forms) (*cont.*)
  secondary sources, 93
  volume numbers and note
    forms, 90
  see also Bibliographic entries;
    Electronic sources; Evalua-
    tion; Note forms
Periods (punctuation), uses of,
  38–39
Personal communication, *see*
  Interviews
Personal research goals, 5
Photocopies (for note-taking),
  13
Plagiarism, **1**:
  and common knowledge,
    16–17
  definition of, 15–16
  quotations to avoid,
    16, 17
  and source materials,
    17–20
  types of, 15
Planning, **1h**:
  objectives (stated) and, 20
  outlines and, 20–21
  reviewing notes during, 20
  thesis statements and, 20
Postings (online)
  bibliographic entries for,
    146
  note forms for, 110
Prefaces
  bibliographic entries for,
    139
  as elements of papers, 127
  note forms for, 85
Primary sources
  bibliographic entries for, 88
  definition of, 88, 93
  note forms for, 88, 93
Print sources, *see* Books; Evalu-
    ation; Periodicals; Sepa-
    rately published materials
Printed texts (for note-taking),
  13
Proceedings (from a conference)
  bibliographic entries for, 139
  note forms for, 86
Professional research goals, 4

Prose quotations
  brief, 72
  long, 73
Pseudonyms, authors using,
  70, 79, 136
Publication
  facts of, 64
  and note forms, 64
Publishers
  shortened forms for,
    64–65
  and source evaluation, 9
  and note forms, 64
Punctuation
  brackets, 44, 75
  colons, 40–41
  commas, 39–40
  dashes, 42–43
  ellipsis points, 45–46, 76
  exclamation points, 42
  hyphens, 42
  parentheses, 43
  periods, 38–39
  in note forms, 65
  with note numbers, 63
  question marks, 41
  quotation marks, 45
  with quotations, 74–76
  revision and, 24
  semicolons, 40
  slashes, 44, 72
  of titles, 65
  see also Mechanics

Question marks, uses of, 41
Quotation marks
  with brief quotations, 45
  single, 45, 74–75
  uses of, 45
Quotations, **4m**:
  brackets with, 75
  brief, 72–73
  ellipsis points with, 76
  incorporating, 71–74
  long, 73–74
  note-taking and, 15
  punctuation with, 74–76
  prose, 72, 73
  revisions and, 24

in sample paper, 115
single quotation marks with,
74
verbs to introduce, 72
verse, 72–73, 74

Racial bias (word choice),
59–60
Radio broadcasts, *see* Broadcasts (radio)
Recordings
bibliographic entries
for, 142
note forms for, 96–97
source evaluation and, 10
Reference area, in library, 5
Reference works
bibliographic entries for, 138
articles in, note forms for, 82
and note forms, 82
Reference works (online), articles in
bibliographic entries for, 145
note forms for, 106
Reprinted books
bibliographic entries for, 137
note forms for, 80
Research goals, **1c:**
course-related, 3–4
personal, 5
professional, 4
Research methods, **1d:**
internet-based, 8–9
library-based, 5–6
using online catalogs, 6–7
using periodical databases,
6–9
Retrieval information (for electronic sources) and note
forms, 101–102
Retrieval statements, (online)
in note forms, 106
Reviews
bibliographic entries for, 141
elements of, 31
note forms for, 92
Revised works
bibliographic entries for, 137
note forms for, 80

Revision
content and, 23
quotations and, 24
style and, 23–24
technical matters and, 24

Sacred writings
bibliographic entries for, 140
note forms for, 87
Sample paper,
with end notes, 111–126
with footnotes, 133–135
Scholarly projects (online)
bibliographic entries for, 143
definition of, 102
note forms for, 102, 103
Secondary sources
bibliographic entries for, 140,
142
definition of, 88, 93
note forms for, 88, 93
Selections in edited collections
bibliographic entries for,
137–138
note forms for, 81
Semicolons, uses of, 40
Sentence-style capitalization,
46
Separately published materials
(note forms)
brochures, 86
dissertations, 86–87
pamphlets, 86
proceedings (of a confer-
ence), 86
Series, and note forms, 64
Series (works in a)
bibliographic entries for, 138
note forms for, 82
Serif fonts, 34
Slashes
with poetry, 72
uses of, 44
Slide programs
bibliographic entries for, 142
note forms for, 95
Sources
combinations of, 12–13, 23
diversity of, 12

Sources (*cont.*)
  multiple notes from, 66–67
  primary, 88, 93
  secondary, 88, 93
  varied perspectives and, 12
  see also Evaluation
Spacing, *see* Line spacing
Special collections, in library, 6
Specificity (in word choice), 59
Speeches
  bibliographic entries for, 143
  note forms for, 98
  and source evaluation, 10
Speeches, transcripts of (on-line)
  bibliographic entries for, 145
  note forms for, 107
Stacks (bookcases), in library, 5
States (of publication)
  abbreviations of, 129–130
  and note forms, 64
Style
  agreement and, 55–57
  evaluation of sources by, 10
  revision and, 23–24
  transitions and, 53–54
  verb tense and, 54–55
Subject classifications, and on-line catalogs, 7
Subjects
  assessing, 1–2
  narrowing to topics, 2
Submitting a manuscript, 36–37
Summaries (and note-taking), 14–15

Tables
  bibliographic entries for, 143
  elements of, 29
  as elements of papers, 29–31
  format for, 30
  lists of, 29
  note forms for, 99
  and source evaluation, 10
  sample, 132
  spacing and, 30
  titles for, 30

Tables, lists of
  as elements of papers, 26, 127
  format for, 29
  sample, 131
Tables of contents, as elements of papers, 127
Tables (online)
  bibliographic entries for, 145
  note forms for, 108
Technical matters
  revision and, 24
  writing and, 22
Television broadcasts, *see* Broadcasts (television)
Territories, abbreviations of, 129–130
Text (body) of paper, 31, 128
Thesis statements
  definition of, 2–3
  elements of,
  planning and, 20
  revision and, 23
  writing and, 22
Title pages
  author's names and, 25
  as elements of papers, 25, 26, 127
  format for, 25
  publishing information and, 64
  in sample paper, 111
  titles and, 25
Titles
  capitalization and, 47
  and online catalogs, 6
  of papers, 25, 31, 36
  and periodical databases, 7
  and note-taking 14
  and note forms, 63, 65
  revision and, 23
Topics
  narrowing, 2
  strategies for limiting, 2
Transcripts (online)
  bibliographic entries for, 143
  note forms for, 98

Transitions
    editorial style and, 53–54
    revising and, 23
    writing and, 22
Translations, note forms for, 83–84
Translators, and note forms, 64

University presses and note forms, 64
URLs
    definition of, 8
    and note forms, 102
    for source evaluation, 11

Verb tenses, editorial style and, 54–55
Verbs (to introduce quotations), 72
Verse quotations
    brief, 72–73
    long, 74
Volume numbers
    and periodical databases, 7
    and note forms, 64, 90

Web sites (Professional)
    bibliographic entries for, 143
    definition of, 8, 102
    elements of, 102
    evaluation of, 10–12
    kinds of, 8, 102
    note forms for, 102, 103
Word choice, **3c:**
    biased language, 59–61
    colloquialisms, 58–59
    jargon, 58
    noun clusters, 58
    revision and, 23
    specificity, 59
Works in collections, note forms for, 81
Writing
    general strategies for, 21–22
    revision and, 23
    strategies for drafting, 22–23
    style and source evaluations, 10

Years (of publication)
    on copyright page, 64
    in note forms, 64

Format for Chicago-Style Note Forms

1. Indent the first line five spaces; place the note number on the line, followed by a period and one space.
2. List author's names in normal order.
3. Cite the complete title, including subtitles.
4. Separate elements of the note with commas.
5. Include facts of publication in parentheses.
6. Single-space notes; double-space between them.

See Chapters 4–8 for additional information and examples.

Sample Note Forms

A Book by One Author (5a)

1. Milada Anna Vachudová, *Europe Undivided: Democracy, Leverage, and Integration after Communism* (New York: Oxford University Press, 2005), 292.

A Book by Four or More Authors (5c)

1. Susan Martin Tucker et al., *Patient Care Standards: Collaborative Planning and Nursing Interventions,* 7th ed. (St. Louis: Mosby-Yearbook, 2000), 448.

An Edition Other than the First (5g)

1. *Forging the American Character: Readings in United States History,* ed. John R. M. Wilson, 4th ed. (Upper Saddle River, NJ: Prentice, 2003), 83.

A Selection in an Edited Collection (5l)

1. J. Bruce Jacobs, "'Taiwanization' in Taiwan's Politics," in *Cultural, Ethnic, and Political Nationalism in Contemporary Taiwan,* ed. John Makeham and A-Chin Hsiau, 17–54 (New York: Palgrave, 2005), 21.

An Article in an Encyclopedia or Other Reference Work (5n)

1. *The New Grove Dictionary of Music and Musicians,* 2001 ed., s.v. "Salieri, Antonio" (by Rudolf Angermüller).

An Article in a Journal with Continuous Paging (6a)

1. Sally Bick, "*Of Mice and Men:* Copland, Hollywood, and American Musical Modernism," *American Music* 23 (2005): 426.